Teaching Notes on Piano Exam Pieces 2013 & 2014

Grades 1–7

TIMOTHY BARRATT
STEPHEN ELLIS
JULIAN HELLABY
MARGARET MURRAY McLEOD
ANTHONY WILLIAMS

Teaching Notes on Piano Exam Pieces 2013 & 2014

Grades 1–7

With an introduction by JOHN HOLMES, Chief Examiner

ABRSM

First published in 2012 by
ABRSM (Publishing) Ltd, a wholly owned subsidiary of ABRSM

ISBN: 978 1 84849 439 8

AB 3676

A CIP catalogue for this book is available from The British Library.

Typeset by Hope Services (Abingdon) Ltd
Printed in England by Page Bros Ltd, Norwich

CONTENTS

NOTES ON CONTRIBUTORS

Timothy Barratt, ARAM GRSM LRAM ARCM LMusTCL, studied at the Royal Academy of Music and in Paris with Vlado Perlemuter. A solo pianist, accompanist and chamber music player, he also has considerable experience of teaching at all levels. Previously a lecturer and vocal coach at the RAM and TCL, he is now Head of Keyboard at Dulwich College and a teacher at the Junior Academy. He is an ABRSM examiner, trainer, consultant moderator and presenter, and a mentor for the Certificate of Teaching.

Stephen Ellis, Hon GRSM LRAM LGSM ARCM, studied piano and accompaniment at the Royal Academy of Music and has performed extensively in the UK and abroad. He is an experienced piano teacher of all levels, and as a vocal coach he has worked with many distinguished singers. He adjudicates and is an examiner, trainer, moderator and presenter for ABRSM, working internationally in most capacities.

Julian Hellaby, PhD MMus BMus LRAM ARAM, studied piano at the Royal Academy of Music and has performed throughout the UK and overseas. He is an ABRSM examiner, trainer, moderator and public presenter, as well as a mentor for the ABRSM's Certificate of Teaching course. He has extensive experience of piano teaching at all levels, and is currently Associate Research Fellow at Coventry University. He has released six CDs, and his book *Reading Musical Interpretation* was published by Ashgate in 2009.

Margaret Murray McLeod, ARAM FTCL LRAM ARCM, studied piano and composition at the Royal Academy of Music. As well as performing as a soloist and accompanist, she has many years' experience of teaching at all levels. From 1972 she trained student teachers and performers at Edinburgh Napier University, where she was Senior Lecturer for Performance Studies until 1997. Her work as a lecturer, examiner and adjudicator has taken her worldwide.

Anthony Williams, MMus Dip.RAM GRSM LRAM, has an active performing, teaching and adjudicating career in the UK and abroad and is currently Head of Keyboard and Instrumental Music at Radley College, Oxfordshire. He is an examiner (jazz and classical), trainer and moderator for ABRSM as well as a mentor for the Certificate of Teaching. He is the compiler of *Fingerprints,* a collection of original repertoire for piano, and the *Best of Grade* series for piano, and editor of *Simply Classics* (all published by Faber Music).

INTRODUCTION

Choosing new pieces is always exciting – rather like setting out on a journey to somewhere you haven't been before. As a teacher, you are presented with an opportunity to match your students' skills and preferences to the right music for them, while also making use of your teacherly expertise to ensure the right degree of 'stretch and challenge' – as they say in schools! This book is intended to help guide you in making good decisions, together with your student, about which pieces will work most successfully. It sets out to provide useful insights into each piece, which we hope will support you and your students on your teaching and learning journeys.

The expert contributors are all experienced teachers and ABRSM examiners, so they are able to draw upon their interconnected knowledge and understanding gained in each of these contexts. The depth of their expertise enables them to provide valuable hints and tips, as well as helpful advice on how to get the best from the partnership between music and performer: the composer and the student.

In fact, the choice of piece is only the first in an almost never-ending series of choices which becomes the learning journey I mentioned at the beginning. Whether it's Bach, Beethoven or Bartók, Purcell, Poulenc or Peterson, a whole range of decisions – conscious and subconscious – will need to be made in order for the developing pianist to arrive at their destination, in this case, the exam performance. Tempo, touch, fingering, pedalling, phrasing ... the list of choices goes on, so perhaps it would be helpful here to talk about how the decision-making process might be approached.

It is crucial to note that there is no 'ABRSM way' of playing any of our piano exam pieces, although of course there *is* an 'ABRSM way' of assessing how they are played. This is by considering the overall musical outcome – in effect, the cumulative result of all the various musical and technical decisions that will have been made in preparing the performance. For example, ABRSM examiners don't assess fingering, but we do comment on and evaluate its effects, such as evenness of tone or regularity of delivery, which are so often partly the result of fingering choices. Examiners are listening and looking for the degree of skill a candidate shows in controlling the various elements of musical performance, which develop gradually during their learning and practice prior to the exam.

As musicians we are often presented with a range of sources, and it can be a puzzle to establish what the true content of each piece really is. In this case we have the printed scores, the ABRSM recordings and these *Teaching Notes* and, in fact, there is 'truth' in all these sources. Each presents a different perspective on the same thing; the scores being a notated record of what was written by the composer and later published in our edition, the recordings presenting realized performances of the music and the *Teaching Notes* adding various ideas relating to interpretation. There may well be differences between what the scores imply, what the recordings present and what these *Teaching Notes* recommend – but in reality they do not so much contradict as complement each other.

That's the excitement of every musical journey – there will always be a variety of routes to a successful musical result, and our examiners do not assess candidates according to any particular one; instead they judge the combined effectiveness of the various musical performance decisions you and your student have made, taken as a whole. This means that every candidate can play to their strengths, not only in their particular choice of pieces, but also in the way that they interpret them. For example, there is a range of tempos – a working 'bandwidth' of speeds – at which any given piece can successfully be played. For some pieces this will be wider than for others, but even where a metronome mark is given, there is usually room for some flexibility of approach. The examiner will not be assessing the speed of playing absolutely or in isolation, but rather in conjunction with other elements of performance, such as note accuracy and rhythmic character. The right tempo choice for each student is best determined as part of a comfortable balance between it and other elements, so that one element is not sacrificed to another; precision sacrificed to speed, for example.

Between them, the ABRSM scores, recordings and *Teaching Notes* are intended to open a variety of doorways to interpretation. Although these publications are the result of considerable research, drawn from contributors with a wealth of experience, none of our resources can portray and communicate everything within the music. We would like to encourage you to inspire your students to play with creativity and individuality, leading them to achieve successful performances that suit and reflect their particular skills, strengths and enthusiasms. In effect, there needs to be a collaborative partnership between you and each of your students, as they learn how best to portray the composer's musical ideas in their own personal way.

Right through from Grade 1 to Grade 8, each list of pieces, A, B and C, will tend to prioritize certain aspects of piano playing by focusing broadly upon a particular style or group of styles:

List A contains music which generally calls for emphasis on definition of finger-work, clarity of articulation, control of co-ordination, management of texture and (often) ornaments. Part-playing will often feature in List A at the higher grades, where the skill of balancing the various lines of voices effectively will be brought under the spotlight.

List B pieces are particularly likely to call for tonal warmth, expressive shaping, sensitive phrasing and a sense of melody, since they are mostly in Classical and Romantic styles. Cantabile tone will be needed for melodic lines here, as a feeling for phrase structure becomes more central to a convincing performance. Pedalling will be necessary for many of these works, especially those requiring legato effects and richer sonorities. As the grades progress, List B pieces often also call for an ability to manage tempo with a greater degree of flexibility, leading eventually to the need for balanced rubato – musical 'give and take' within the basic pulse. The musical mood and personality of List B pieces will also highlight the candidate's ability to control dynamic changes smoothly and, especially at more advanced grades, to mould and colour the tone in order to enhance the necessary stylistic hallmarks.

List C offers the widest range of styles, and here there is ample opportunity to find something to suit every student. You will find this especially by exploring the many pieces that are not published in the graded volumes. The pieces, which often involve jazzy rhythms and harmonies, can be highly appealing to students and therefore a strong motivation to practise! List C pieces will tend to emphasize subtleties of touch, idiomatic inflections and embellishments, but perhaps above all, the need to project a clear sense of musical identity and character. Quite often here the scope for interpretive decisions is considerable; straight or swing quavers, for example. Once again there is no single right way to play these pieces, and the best eventual result will arise from a well-judged match between each individual candidate's piano skills, and the particular demands of the chosen piece.

It is worth reiterating that examiners will assess the musical outcome heard on the day; the musical effectiveness of the live performance in the exam room – this is at the heart of ABRSM's work.

Candidates can choose the order in which they play their three pieces, and whether to start the exam with these or another element. Once again there is no single right way; as with so much of the musical learning journey leading up to the performance, the exam itself starts with a decision!

We do hope that you will feel excited and inspired by the huge range of musical possibilities open to you and your students within the 2013 & 2014 ABRSM Piano syllabus. Spanning around 400 years of composition, whether it's Rameau or Rebello, there is truly something for everyone to embark upon and enjoy.

John Holmes

GRADE 1

Students will usually have been learning for up to eighteen months by the time Grade 1 is on the horizon. They may have taken the Prep Test during this time, in which case they will probably feel quite confident when facing their first graded exam. A wide choice of pieces should help to keep motivation high, so why not have some alternatives prepared, then choose the best three as the exam approaches? The criteria for assessment for all grades are printed in *These Music Exams* – a useful source of reference for teachers.

A:1 Mozart *Minuet in G*

It is humbling to consider that Mozart was younger than the majority of music exam candidates when he composed this elegant, finely-crafted dance! The confident phrasing and attractive melodic shape have a maturity and sophistication which can be enjoyed by students of all ages.

The tempo should be sufficiently dignified and unhurried to evoke the gestures of this courtly dance, yet the quaver anacrusis and hairpins must always provide a sense of forward movement. Gently shaped tone and a mixture of detached and slurred crotchets will give poise to the opening two-bar phrases. Fuller tone will point the shift to D major over bars 5–6 and the somewhat irregular phrasing can be punctuated by detaching the right-hand crotchets. A confident sense of keyboard geography and disciplined fingering will ensure accurate left-hand leaps throughout. Inventing words to fit the rhythm may help to space the triplet evenly in bar 7 and, as always, students should make sure that the short trill does not interrupt the flow.

The musical content of the second half remains similar to that of the first. Practising the 'join' at the double bar, anticipating the leaps, will help to eliminate any hesitation as both hands move upwards. Further variety may be achieved by beginning *mp* and playing the second phrase as an echo, an effective alternative to the editorial dynamics marked.

A:2 Rowley *Fugue*

Fugues are usually associated with more advanced players, but here is a charming, well-crafted example perfect for introducing contrapuntal style to your student. The notes are relatively straightforward due to few changes of hand-position, and there are no tricky rhythms to negotiate.

A bold, rhythmically defined three-bar 'subject' will immediately establish the serious, Bach-like character. Establishing a magisterial tempo, which allows no hint of rushing, is fundamental to a successful performance. Some preliminary five-finger exercises, practising the semiquaver groups ascending and descending, will help articulation and pacing to remain even in both hands. Detaching the repeated quavers in bar 2 and in subsequent appearances of the subject will add contrast to the otherwise smooth line and a slight diminuendo in the following bar will make way for the left hand's entrance with its equally bold 'answer'.

The shift to *piano* and left-hand couplet phrasing across the bar-line at bar 7 provide a welcome change of mood. Fingering needs care here, and the first left-hand note in bar 11 should be detached in order to re-sound in the right hand. Your student can decide either to play a *subito forte* at bar 13 or to make a crescendo towards *forte* in bar 12 (both work well), and shouldn't miss the imitation between the hands in bar 18. Firm, well-paced quavers, with the last bar held for its full length, will sustain the serious mood until the end.

A:3 Türk *Das Ballett*

The sense of fun in this lively, cheerful music gives it instant appeal to students who enjoy athletic pieces. In addition to its musical attraction, the piece provides the perfect vehicle for developing neatness and agility.

Choosing a tempo which can be maintained throughout is determined largely by the semiquavers after the double bar-line. Although the majority of the piece is marked *forte*, the tone should be bright, not heavy, in order to capture the light-hearted style, and always with a sense of rise and fall within each phrase. A light hand staccato will give clarity and buoyancy to the repeated notes, and definition can be given to the rhythm by a slight accent on the first beat of the bar. Slurring the quavers in couplets in bar 3 would provide relief from the largely detached quaver phrasing.

There must be no change of tempo as the music takes a somewhat more athletic turn after the double bar-line. Maintaining evenness in the semiquavers at this point while ensuring that the hands play exactly together is likely to pose the main challenge of the piece. Slow, meticulous right-hand practice, lifting each finger cleanly, will help to develop that all-important control of the weaker fingers. Legato left-hand quavers may be the less fussy option here and a sufficiently quiet *piano*, with the short phrases separated, will make the most of the echo.

A:4 Neefe *Minuetto in G*

All the grace and stately elegance of the eighteenth century seems to be encapsulated in this charming, little-known minuet. The right hand moves almost entirely in scalic patterns and the piece's measured tempo and rests should allow time to find the left-hand shapes safely and easily.

The 16 bars of the piece are formed of four phrases of equal length. A slight 'breath' at the end of each will punctuate the phrasing in both hands, except perhaps in bar 12, in which the left-hand quavers may flow naturally towards the following bar. Carefully paced quavers, with all fingers lifted precisely, will ensure clean lines, and smooth thumb movement will avoid any unwanted bumps in tone.

The absence of any dynamic indications provides considerable scope for exploring one's own ideas. Each four-bar phrase has its own natural rise and fall, and ends of phrases can be elegantly tapered. Any extreme tonal contrasts would be somewhat out of place in this gentle, refined music; however, the shift to A minor at bar 9 seems to suggest a more robust dynamic level than elsewhere. A drop to *piano* would also be an effective option.

Similarly, most phrasing choices are left to the performer. Detached crotchets will give a measured step to the rhythm and contrast effectively with the smoother quavers. The trills in bars 7 and 15 may be played as four- or five-note turns starting on either A or B, although three-note upper mordents are acceptable.

A:5 Purcell *Prelude*

Although only ten bars long, this wonderful piece contains a wealth of expressive detail to be savoured. Its shifting harmonies created by the undulating quaver movement seem to have a timeless quality which will be appreciated by sensitive students.

The right hand moves mainly in triadic blocks, with rests enabling the shift between positions. The complementary left hand is more sustained, and some overlapping of the quavers here might further enhance the harmonies. However, the right-hand rests should be carefully observed in order to avoid any clash when the harmonies change at the half-bar.

Organized fingering will allow the longer bass notes to be sustained for their full value, and lovely suspensions can be created if the thumb holds the 'tenor' line for as long as possible before moving upwards to the next note in bars 8–9.

Thinking in minim beats will allow the piece to flow unhindered by any unwanted accents. The undulating rise and fall of the figuration serves as a guideline for discovering the musical shape, with any inflection always gentle and subtle. Tapering the groups of four right-hand quavers will add further refinement to the phrasing. The highest peak occurs at bar 6 after which the tone might diminish towards the ending. The realization of the ornament in bar 9 may be simplified from the suggested four demisemiquavers to two semiquavers.

A:6 Wagenseil *Courtly Dance*

The title sums up the graceful character of this dance with its stately rhythmic steps and regular phrase structure. It offers opportunities for sensitive tonal shaping and must be underpinned by a steady sense of pulse throughout.

A well-defined opening dotted figure, followed by lighter second and third beats, will immediately establish the minuet rhythm. The slurs in bar 3 can be lightly detached and a tapered finish to bar 4 will highlight the implied imperfect cadence. It may be effective to make a slightly louder start to the second main phrase at bar 5. Inventing words for the rhythmic pattern in bar 7 may help to produce an evenly spaced triplet. Confident rhythmic spacing is also needed in the following bar in order to avoid the common error of adding an extra beat at the end of sections!

Care should be taken not to change speed as the left hand switches to quaver patterns at bar 9. The hands have identical phrasing for much of the piece, but at this point good independence is needed to punctuate the rests while maintaining smooth left-hand quavers. The suggested echo effect will work well if the *piano* bars are sufficiently quiet and the left hand accompanies throughout.

Again there must be no rhythmic 'gear change' at the start of the final four bars. However, a small, evenly-paced ritardando will round off the piece effectively.

B:1 Gedike *Moderato*

The crisp articulations and dotted rhythms give a distinctive quality to this music, which also offers the opportunity to focus on combining legato and staccato touch. Since the approach to the dynamics can be quite robust, the piece is a good one to start with (in the exam candidates may perform the pieces in the order of their choice). The two accents marked in bars 2 and 10 must be prominent but need to lighten onto the following quaver E. Similarly, the other slurred notes and phrase-endings require careful tapering as well.

There are few changes in hand-position and the fingering provided should enable the student to maintain a rounded hand-shape. In bar 8 it would be advisable to take the left hand's third quaver with finger 3 (as marked) in order that consistency is maintained in bar 9 as the opening phrase reappears.

Bars 4 and 12 should be precisely counted, and slow isolated practice will be required to ensure that the dotted-quaver/semiquaver figure in the left hand co-ordinates exactly with the fourth semiquaver in the right. Students should be attentive to the left-hand quaver rests; the performance will lose some of its bite otherwise.

The moderato speed gives the music an almost regal character, slightly reminiscent of a medieval courtly dance with a drum underpinning the beat. The *Capriol Suite* by Peter Warlock might offer some useful associated listening.

B:2 Swinstead *Sailor's Song*

This jovial piece is in fact a hornpipe. Favourable comparisons might be drawn from elsewhere, including the Hornpipe by Purcell which is set for Grade 2. One might imagine a bustling harbour with the sailors merrily going about their chores in excited anticipation of a forthcoming voyage.

Legato and staccato touches need to be clearly defined and some challenges may be met when the two are combined. The left-hand crotchets require a gentle bounce and the right hand's slurred offbeat crotchets in bars 9–11 and 15–16 should not be unduly accented. These bars possibly describe the straining of ropes and rigging of sails.

The dynamics are clear and self-explanatory, mainly offering strong changes between *forte* and *piano*, but the crescendo beginning in bar 9 must start *piano* in order to be able to swell to the highest point of *forte* in bar 12. Tonal gradation combined with the implied syncopation might cause rushing, so the beat will need to be carefully anchored! A ritardando, however tempting, is not advisable here, since rhythmic momentum would be compromised.

A brisk but unhurried approach to the music will help to convey its cheerful dance character. A whisper of delay over the last bar would give the final accented chord extra aplomb.

B:3 Rybicki *Na łódce (In a Boat)*

This affectionate, intimate piece will suit the more sensitive student. The main challenge lies in conveying the music's lilting simplicity, for which an almost seamless legato is required in both hands.

Although the melody is divided into two-bar phrases, thinking in phrases of four will help to avoid cumbersome accentuation. To maintain the flow the third-beat quaver in bars 2, 6, 10 and 14 should be only very gently detached or lifted. Singing these phrases, at a comfortable vocal range, is the best way to internalize the music.

More expressive intensity would be welcome at bar 9 and the crescendo in bars 9–10 should be subtly graded or the effect will be lost. The *mezzo-forte* direction here would be a good point at which to encourage the practice of cantabile; this might then be extended into the softer playing.

Practising the left hand as block chords will bring familiarization and also help hand-position. It is a good idea to think of the middle note of each triad as a pivot, 'suspending' one chord to the next. When quavers are re-introduced, a relaxed rotary wrist movement should aid fluency. Good balance between the hands will be expected, and in the initial learning stages it would be worthwhile experimenting with a louder dynamic in the right hand.

The gentle rocking motion gradually subsides when, with a carefully paced rallentando, the boat reaches the shoreline.

B:4 Borodin *Polovtsian Dance*

This well-known melody, originally from Borodin's opera *Prince Igor*, will be recognized instantly as it has been widely used in other genres, including in the musical *Kismet*.

Thinking of the broad melodic lines – moving forward, the rest treated as a breath mark – will serve to maintain the line and flow. The bare intervals of the descending 4th and the ascending 5th complement the mostly stepwise movement found elsewhere. Legato needs to be carefully managed and blended, especially when the melody is divided between the hands in bars 7 and 15; this needs a fluid transition from one hand to the other.

Expressive markings need particular attention throughout in order to give shape to the phrases. Dynamics will need to be exploited fully, since the range is fairly wide (*ppp–più forte*). The left hand is relatively straightforward; however, careful tapering and attentive listening will be needed on the semitone/tone descent over bars 3–4 (C–B), 5–6 (B–A) and 7–8 (A–G♯), and in the reprise of the melody. The rests in the left hand could be easily overlooked, so attention should be drawn to these.

The expansive Russianness of the music wants to be savoured, and the touches of direct pedalling indicated will add tonal warmth and give fluency to the syncopated rhythms. A stressed second beat should be avoided; the 'dreamy' mood might be compromised otherwise.

B:5 Gurlitt *Die Klappermühle (Clappermill)*

The *sempre staccato* quavers, which are strongly evocative of the monotonous clattering of the mill's wheel, need a crisp, incisive touch throughout. Crotchet = *c*.96 would be a judicious tempo, giving a suitably mechanical motion to the music and allowing the fingers to find the notes comfortably. The hand shape should be rounded with the fingers playing on their tips, and the wrists pliable, employing a slight lateral movement in order to discourage any possible tension.

The four-bar phrases should be free from accents, and at a level dynamic. Any sense of crescendo or diminuendo would detract from the desired percussive effect. The changes in dynamic, however, need to be clearly contrasted, with a bolder minor section in bars 9–16 and a strong *forte* finish.

Alternative fingerings for the right-hand 3rds in bars 9–10 might be 5/1-4/2, and for the 6ths in bars 13–14, 5/2-4/1; these will be dependent on the shape or size of the student's hand. The left-hand fingering in bars 13–14 where the second finger crosses over the first is a sensible approach to take. Encourage a little rotary wrist movement here and also in the following two bars (15–16), where the quavers will need some isolated separate-hand practice.

This is a humorous piece, full of character, which is also a splendid study in staccato.

B:6 F. Wohlfahrt *Allegretto*

A tempo of crotchet = 136 would ideally suit the lyrical nature of this charming piece. There should be a sense of one-in-a-bar, but without any feeling of agitation or hurrying; only if there is sufficient poise will the *grazioso* character emerge convincingly. The arabesque-like quaver upbeat figurations want to lead delicately into the tenuto dotted crotchets. A lovely cantabile quality is to be encouraged here, using the three quavers to give the necessary impetus. There should be no hint of accent, though, as this would labour rhythmic flow and stifle the musical line.

A lilting dance-like feel can be achieved by employing a suitably light touch. The left hand's articulation needs to be carefully followed throughout. A gentle bounce on the staccato quavers in bars 1–7 will give the momentum for the leap to the second beat, but care must be taken to avoid accents.

The piece's second half has a slightly less sprightly feel and tapering in the legato quavers is required; rests, however, should be meticulously observed. For the more adventurous, pedal could be attempted at the start of each bar, lifting after the third quaver. The pedalling might need to change slightly according to the conditions, so practice is recommended on different pianos and in varying acoustics.

Finally, a tiny ritenuto will bring the piece to a sedate and graceful close.

C:1 Richard Rodney Bennett *Thursday*

It is never too soon to start learning about modes and, in this piece for white keys only, one must be careful not to play F♯s to ensure the Mixolydian flavour.

For a Grade 1 student the 3rds may be challenging. To help master these, you can encourage your student to practise dropping the hands onto a flat surface, tilting the arm outwards slightly towards finger 5 as contact with the surface is made, then rotating gently inwards, ensuring that finger 3 is repeated. This motion, once mastered, can then be transferred to the appropriate notes on the keyboard. In bars 4 and 12, fingering the first chord 2/1 may aid a legato link from the melodic quaver B at the end of the preceding bars.

The entire piece is marked *piano*, except for the last two bars in which use of the *una corda* pedal may enhance the *pianissimo*. However, some dynamic shading can add musical interest; in bars 7–8, for example, a slight crescendo to *mezzo-piano* by halfway through bar 8 followed by *subito piano* on the final quaver could prove effective. Also, a ritenuto from the fifth quaver of bar 12 to the end would add an appropriate sense of conclusion.

It would be interesting to find out how many of your students can connect the mood of this piece to that of their typical Thursday!

C:2 Shostakovich *March*

The sturdy rhythms of this piece might conjure up the image of Russian soldiers on the march, but the humorous 'wrong note' sections in the middle and at the end perhaps imply toy soldiers, not to be taken too seriously!

The suggested metronome setting of crotchet = *c.*168 provides a suitable tempo although it might be advisable to think of this as minim = *c.*84 to match the mainly two-in-a-bar march feeling of the left hand. The pulse should be rock steady throughout and no rubato is needed. In a piece such as this, practising to the tick of a metronome may well be beneficial; this is particularly the case when the dynamic is *piano* because less experienced pianists can sometimes lose speed when playing quietly. However, the marked dynamics are editorial and there are possible alternatives. For example, bars 9–12 could be played *forte* throughout and then echoed *piano* in bars 13–16. A crescendo in the last two bars also seems appropriate.

A generally firm touch from well-rounded fingers will provide some clear articulation in the right hand. A relaxed but rhythmic down–up left forearm motion will help to define the march rhythm and provide tonal support without overwhelming the right-hand part.

Playing this piece to your younger students could also provide an ideal opportunity for some helpful 'music and movement'.

C:3 Harry Warren and Mack Gordon *Chattanooga Choo Choo*

For a good lesson in swing style, it may be advisable for your student to listen to one of the 1940s big bands, such as the Glenn Miller Orchestra, playing this tune.

Crotchet = *c.*112 yields a suitably solid tempo, although nimble Grade 1 students could raise this to *c.*128 for a more lively account. Once established, however, the beat must remain stable. The swung quavers should not sound too polite and some gentle offbeat accents may enhance the performance style. For example, the right-hand and left-hand Gs in bar 2 can both be slightly emphasized.

When your student adopts the opposing articulations indicated in places such as bar 3, the necessary playing sensation can be practised firstly on a table-top where a right-hand finger (maybe 5) touches and maintains contact with the surface while a left-hand finger (maybe 1) simultaneously touches and is then instantly raised from the surface. This exercise can then be transferred to the relevant notes on the keyboard (for example G in the right hand over middle C in the left) before the whole passage is attempted.

Following the suggested phrasing and dynamics will benefit the musical shape of the piece although the touch need not be especially legato, given the jaunty nature of the music. After all, it needs to swing along merrily!

C:4 Elias Davidsson *The Merry Bagpipe*

This lively bagpipe impression, with its drone and weirdly off-key melody, makes no great technical demands. The left hand stays in a five-finger position until the last bar and the right hand moves around only very slightly more.

The music can go at a good allegro pace, in the region of dotted crotchet = 108, retaining a stable, unvarying pulse throughout. Clapping of both the pulse and the rhythms can help to develop the required steadiness.

Four dynamic levels are marked and these can be practised outside the context of the piece – perhaps using a scale. Scale monitoring could then be made more interesting if you ask your student to play a certain scale at one of the four dynamic levels. Even better, your student could select a dynamic level and then ask you to guess which has been chosen. The marked articulation is predominantly legato but fingers need to be lifted well clear of the key to enable the amount of drop necessary for producing the *forte* tone that is called for much of the time. The staccato chords in bars 10 and 12 demand active fingertips and a firm but flexible wrist.

The older or inquisitive-minded learner might like to know that the music uses the Lydian flat seven mode: 'Lydian' because the 4th (G) is sharpened, and 'flat seven' – well, guess!

C:5 Heather Hammond *Cowboy Lullaby*

Imagine a cowboy dozing under a tree with his hat shading his face and his horse grazing nearby, and you will get the gist of this piece.

The composer suggests a metronome mark of dotted crotchet = 60, although raising this to *c.*72 retains the desired drowsiness and gives the music slightly more sense of direction. Whatever tempo is adopted, hurrying should be avoided at all costs and, to develop the appropriate feeling, your student could move slowly round the room in time to your performance of the piece.

The touch needs to be legato throughout, practice for which can be integrated with work on scales and broken chords. The dynamic markings at the beginning indicate that the left hand should be played slightly more quietly than the right. The left-hand fifth finger hangs on to the bass note of each bar which helpfully restricts the amount of lift possible in the other fingers. The right hand can therefore be freer and held a little higher above the keyboard than the left, although nowhere should the dynamic level exceed *mezzo-forte.*

This piece provides an introduction to the blues in terms of its characteristic use of flattened 7ths and its structure – although you would have to explain that the two-bar introduction makes the piece last for 14 bars rather than 12!

C:6 Fishel Pustilnik *Jay-Walker*

Jay-walkers, as careless pedestrians, may seem rather casual and a certain casualness can be heard in this music, although a successful performance will have been carefully prepared! The music needs to move with an 'easy swing' and a tempo of crotchet = *c.*104 seems to deliver this. Pustilnik has opted to show swung quavers as dotted rhythms – even at Grade 1 it does no harm to realize that there is no consensus concerning swing notation.

The trickiest aspect of this music is its rhythm in which well-placed syncopations and carefully measured rests are crucial. At this level, complex counting systems written onto the score could prove counter-productive and it may be wise to teach the piece by rote, allowing your student to copy and feel the rhythms as played by you or heard on the recording. Once the aural and kinaesthetic aspects have been grasped it might then be appropriate to support this with some theoretical understanding.

The only dynamic level indicated is *mezzo-forte*, though with occasional crescendo/diminuendo modifications. However, there is no harm in adapting this slightly, perhaps applying a diminuendo in bar 11 and returning to *mezzo-forte* for the D major chord in bar 12.

Since much of this piece uses A minor and D major harmonies (derived from the Dorian mode on A), your student might enjoy improvising around these two chords.

GRADE 2

Students may want to play something similar to their favourite piece from their Grade 1 exam, but there is plenty of choice, so do consider all the options. Preparation for all parts of the exam will probably be easier for those who have already achieved success at Grade 1.

A:1 Purcell *Hornpipe*

The better-known movement from Purcell's incidental music to *Abdelazer* is the Rondo which Britten famously used in his *Young Person's Guide to the Orchestra*. This delightful hornpipe has a more rustic, dance-like quality by comparison. It requires lightness of touch, as well as a consistent approach to articulation.

The suggestions in the score are editorial and appropriate alternatives may be found. The original version was for strings so listening to an authentic recording would give the student a real flavour of the style and period. Websites such as YouTube offer an abundance of listening opportunities. It will help when searching to know that this piece is also known as 'Hole in the Wall'. There are two distinct approaches to the articulation. In both, the right hand's quavers are mostly detached; in the left hand all notes could be played smoothly, or the crotchets and quavers could be detached – which might better convey the music's sprightly character.

Dynamics would have been used in the original arrangement and they certainly add colour and interest when played on the piano. The first repeat should be included (i.e. bars 1–4), so contrast in the reprise would be advisable. The changes in general are bold, but a carefully graded crescendo would add shape to the rising sequential passage in bars 9–11.

The ornaments are simple to realize and will definitely add stylistic polish. The longer trill in the final bar should be carefully tapered, and it would be effective to continue the momentum to the end.

A:2 Telemann *Très vite*

Listening to or, better still, playing a harpsichord would help to give a tangible sense of the tonal colour required here. The slightly steely timbre of the instrument gives this dance-like music a faintly rustic flavour, although the actual character is closer to that of a bourrée.

Adopting a duple rather than quadruple metre will help to convey *Très vite* (very quick). This is suggested by the editorial metronome marking and will help to prevent the phrases from becoming laboured or stodgy. There are a few wide intervals to negotiate, but otherwise the music lies quite nicely under the hands. The crotchets, if lightly detached, will help to communicate the style and character. The suggested dynamics, which are editorial markings only, give clear definition to the phrases. A softer and lighter touch would definitely suit the playful interchange between the hands in bars 9–14 and 19–24.

Overall, the approach to the piece needs to be robust, and underpinned by rhythmic drive and energy. There should be no sense of slowing down or holding back until perhaps the last bar where a slight ritardando on the quavers, although not indicated, would add a little elegance to the final curtsy.

A:3 Attwood *Allegro*

What is the point of learning scales, aural and theory? Teachers have the answer, but it adds fuel to the fire if they can present a piece which strengthens the issues and makes the learning process fun. This sparkling Allegro is just such an example. Form, triads with inversions and even 7th notes can all be included in the teaching of this piece. Approaching the lesson holistically can be both satisfying and productive.

You and your student might first look at the right hand's regular four-bar phrases and also analyse the chord structure in the left. The Alberti bass could be played as block triads initially. An investigation of tonic–dominant relationships would give students a harmonic overview. Simple ternary form could also be explored.

Of course, the musical outcome is paramount. A bright, agile approach is needed, but the right hand should have linear flow without over-accentuation. The left-hand figurations will require a gentle rotary wrist movement. Synchronization of the hands in bars 9–16 might be a little problematic, but slow practice will remedy this.

Having now analysed the piece in detail it might be possible for your student to memorize it. Although this is not required for exam performances, successful memorization will give an immense feeling of achievement and satisfaction.

A:4 Duncombe *Giga*

This jaunty cheerful dance has a definite rustic flavour. One can imagine an eighteenth-century barn dance with merry peasants having fun! Since a firm dotted-crotchet lilt is required to give the dancers a spring in their step, the tempo should not be too fast.

There are some angular lines in the left hand, and a lateral wrist movement should be encouraged when turning the thumb under the second or third fingers, for example over bars 7–8. In bars 9 and 10 it is important to change the right-hand fingering from 3/1 to 2/1 in order to make the access to the high C/D as fluent and comfortable as possible. Students with small hands may divide the parts between the hands at bars 9–10, but should return to position in bar 11.

The paired dotted crotchets found throughout the piece should be sensitively tapered. The trills form an integral part of the melodic line and must be even and shapely in their execution. The momentary change of mood in bars 13–16 is almost teasing. More tonal delicacy will be required here and the dynamic change to *piano* will help to reflect this. The acciaccaturas and trills are best played on the beat. In general the ornaments are straightforward and they are essential in delivering a stylistic performance.

A:5 Handel *Menuett in G minor*

The choice of a minor key for this dance gives the music a very regal, stately air and the speed ought to be quite sedate in order to reflect this. There is no tempo indication but a metronome mark suggestion of crotchet = *c.*108 would give the music a suitably unhurried lilt.

One could imagine this being played by two oboes and a bassoon. The Trio from the fourth movement of Bach's first Brandenburg Concerto draws a favourable comparison and might provide an interesting listening opportunity. There is an absence of phrasing, so detaching the crotchets and slurring the quavers would offer a stylistic solution. There are possible alternatives but simplicity and consistency will produce the best results. To achieve complete clarity in the right-hand 3rds the suggested fingering 3/1, 5/3, 3/2 in bar 3 and 3/1, 5/1, 3/2 in bar 7 is recommended. Initially this fingering might appear cumbersome but it is worth the perseverance.

The choice of dynamics should follow a discussion between teacher and student. Experimentation will ultimately produce the desired effect but, again, simplicity is recommended. The music has a slightly melancholic feel so a softer colour might be suitable for bars 1–8 and 19–26, offering the opportunity to provide a real contrast in the middle.

Your student might compare this with other minuets from the period, including those in major keys.

A:6 Haydn *Minuet in B flat*

This charming piece is full of the grace and elegance that one would expect in a minuet by Haydn. Rhythmic poise and real engagement with Classical phrase shaping will lead to a successful and stylish performance. A relatively sedate tempo is needed, for which a metronome guideline of crotchet = 96 would be suitable.

The touch should be light but the triplets require good legato control throughout. The crotchets in bars 5–6 and 13–14 could be played legato, lightly detached, or a combination of slurred and detached – for example, slurring first and second beats, gently lifting on the second beat and lightly detaching the third. The staccato marks in the following bar are then complemented. In turn, this choice of articulation aids the music's lilting character and gives buoyancy to the rhythm. The other important aspect of the phrasing is the feminine ending which is found at bar 12; the right hand's two notes need to be carefully tapered in order to demonstrate this stylistic feature. The dynamic markings cover a good range and they will certainly enhance the performance.

There are no real difficulties here but the opening left-hand interval can be supported by a touch of pedal, and the rests, especially at bars 4 and 12, must be meticulously counted. An intake of breath at these points might help to reinforce this – providing it is quietly done!

B:1 Nicolai Podgornov *Bear Dance*

Here is a piece which is guaranteed to appeal to all teddy-bear lovers – a cuddly, if somewhat gruff, bear entertaining an admiring audience with his dancing. Although there is a mock-seriousness to the heavy, slightly unwieldy movements, the use of the bass register and galumphing rhythms add a comic element to this fine character-piece.

The opening two bars act as an introduction, as the bear positions himself centre-stage, perhaps acknowledging applause on the accented chord. The dance proper, which begins at bar 3, needs firm fingers to give clarity to the left-hand rhythmic detail, at a tempo suited to the ponderous mood. The smooth two-bar phrases suggest slightly cautious, earthbound movements which then contrast with the more athletic feel from bar 11 onwards. Detaching non-slurred quavers and making the most of the second-beat accents at this point will highlight the comedy of the situation.

The accompanying right-hand chords, which should be given their full length, with all notes sounding, contribute towards the ungainly rhythmic character. Co-ordination between the hands needs care, especially when playing the dotted figures, and careful practice will ensure that changes of chord shape are cleanly managed.

Melodic interest shifts to the right hand for the final four bars. Firm, detached chords, with the top note highlighted, will carry the slightly grumpy mood through to the end of the piece.

B:2 Stanford *Lullaby*

The gentle innocence of this lovely piece is guaranteed to rock even the most restless child to sleep! Sensitive tonal control, with the hands well balanced, and an ability to convey the rhythmic lilt are key factors in producing a fine performance.

While initially counting in quavers will ensure that longer notes are given full value, there is no substitute for feeling the pulse in a gentle two-in-a-bar. Sinking into the first of the dotted crotchets and floating gently off the second will help to achieve that all-important rocking motion, a recurring feature throughout the piece. Smooth, controlled quavers, with no unwanted accents, will further enhance the restful character.

Left-hand practice will eliminate any hesitations at changes of hand-position. An effective texture is dependent on holding notes for their full length – for instance, the lower notes in bars 8, 14 and 22 should sustain while the 'tenor' part moves. Care is needed not to replay the tied thumb notes in bars 17–18.

A firm yet gentle *piano* at the start will leave room for a quieter tone as the tonality turns towards minor from bar 5. Depressing the keys fully, listening carefully, will ensure that all notes sound at their quietest levels. The shift to C major heralds the climax at bar 13, after which one can sense the child drifting into slumber as the tone gradually fades towards the end.

B:3 Li Yinghai *Xiong mao (The Panda)*

The timeless quality of this evocative piece with its cosy scene of a panda feeding contentedly on bamboo shoots provides an intriguing and refreshing choice for student and teacher alike. Notes are relatively straightforward, with the left hand moving in 5ths throughout, and the leisurely tempo allows for the changes of register to be negotiated accurately.

A gentle, smooth two-bar introduction will immediately establish a scene of calm contentment. Thereafter the left hand becomes the accompanist to a melodic line whose phrase lengths vary between half a bar and a whole bar, a feature which can be highlighted by a slight 'breath' at the end of each phrase. Although dynamic levels range only between *piano* and *mezzo-forte*, there is ample opportunity for warmth and sensitive shaping within phrases, yet without any exaggeration at the hairpins. The end of each of the 'stanzas' is marked by three half-bar repeated figures, which increase in intensity as they approach the more gentle gong-like 5ths.

Accurately measured rhythmic detail will allow the crotchet pulse to flow calmly and evenly. Particular care is needed to ensure that the right-hand 5th is placed on the half-beat in bar 6 and elsewhere. Optional touches of pedal at these points would add extra resonance to these gong-like figures, which should be sustained for their full length.

B:4 Fly *Grinding the Corn*

This charming piece seems to evoke an image of an era when farming was a gentle, pre-technological occupation. Although this may be far removed from the experience of many modern children, the piece has the appeal of a favourite old toy.

The duple time signature gives a grace and elegance to the music by ensuring that individual crotchets are not emphasized. The tempo should be unhurried, yet with the measured rhythmic patterns creating a sense of movement towards the bar-line. The predominantly staccato touch should always be clear yet light, and the occasional slur adds welcome variety to the phrasing. The suggested pedalling, although not obligatory, will serve to enhance the phrasing; a similarly smooth effect, however, may be achieved by judicious holding-down of the fingers. Perhaps the main technical challenge lies in ensuring that both notes sound together in the right-hand 3rds – slow practice, keeping the hand relaxed, will help this.

The subtle dynamic range, which rarely rises beyond *mezzo-forte*, needs imaginative tonal shading. The *pianissimo* moments are especially effective and stresses serve to underline unexpected notes, for example, the G♭ in bar 3. Activity 'winds down' at a couple of points midway, after which careful pacing is needed for the return to *a tempo*. Full length should be given to the semibreve 3rd in the penultimate bar and the final note played as quietly as possible.

B:5 Glinka *Polka*

Imagining the lively movements and stamping rhythms of a folk dance in the Russian countryside will set the scene for this attractive polka, which is best suited to a student with confident fingers and a strong sense of pulse.

Piano candidates do not have the support of an accompanist, so must develop the skill of setting an appropriate, sustainable tempo unaided. Here the speed should convey the two-in-a-bar dance rhythms, while being sufficiently steady to prevent disaster. Taut rhythm, with no speeding up in the final bars, will hold the poised yet energetic mood throughout.

Careful semiquaver practice, using reliable fingering, especially in the second half, is essential for right-hand confidence. In addition, tailor-made exercises, using fingers 3, 4 and 5, may help to improve control and definition. Explore the suggested finger-changes on repeated notes to add clarity to the phrasing, and take care not to bump the thumb note in bar 12.

Playing sufficiently quietly in the *piano* bars will help to achieve an effective dynamic range. Contrasts should happen suddenly, with the exception of the crescendo in bars 13–14, and the characteristic 'folky' second-beat accents in the first half provide additional musical interest.

The left hand plays a supporting role throughout the piece, providing regular momentum and pacing. Neat synchronization with the faster-moving right-hand melody is important and quiet offbeat chords will highlight the more important 'bass' line.

B:6 Sullivan *Gavotte*

The gently stepping rhythm and stylized phrasing of this charming gavotte seem to evoke the unhurried pace and good manners of a bygone era. Each phrase begins on the third beat of the bar, a feature of this dance, always gently propelling the music towards the next bar-line.

The detailed quaver phrasing dictates the tempo, which should move without any haste. The four-quaver slur/staccato pattern, implying a detached second note of the slur, is a characteristic gesture which occurs throughout the piece. A slight stress on the first note of the slur followed by three light staccato notes will produce a graceful, dainty effect here. Elsewhere the mix of crotchet slurs and staccato is easiest to manage when identical phrasing occurs in both hands.

Little dynamic guidance is provided in the score. Each phrase has its natural rise and fall, always with a sense of the importance of the first beat and lighter subsidiary beats. The brief diversion midway into D minor and F major calls for a change of mood – perhaps quieter and more thoughtful. Busier, more 'flowery' gestures grace the final eight bars, an area likely to need the most practice in order to ensure co-ordination of the hands and measured quavers. A gently tapered final scale will ensure that the graceful character is maintained until the final chord.

C:1 Hanna, Barbera and Curtin *Meet the Flintstones*

Meet the Flintstones, here in glorious pianistic colour! This gem of a tune, in a rock groove, has nostalgic appeal and is great fun. From a teacher's perspective the arrangement wonderfully combines the motivation to practise with technical challenges.

The first challenge is to bring out the melodic line at the top of the right hand, particularly in the chords. Time should be spent developing the necessary technique and control as well as the listening skills to judge the sound. A bold sense of rhythmic drive and solidity is essential; how a note ends is important, as the rests convey rhythmic energy. For instance, in bar 1 the lift of the right-hand C should be clearly defined as soon as the left hand plays F to enhance the syncopated 6th.

Dynamic shading is crucial even where not marked. The piece's first two notes might be phrased off, the middle C lighter than the first chord (as in 'Flintstones'). The quavers in bar 3 could get louder towards the third beat and, despite the uniform tenuto markings, the inner notes in bar 4 could decrease in volume to allow the melodic E through. There are some rhythmic surprises such as the 'Scotch snap' in bars 10 and 12.

The tempo – distinctly four-in-a-bar – should be unhurried, supporting a confident and fun performance. Above all, players should have a 'yabadabadoo' time!

C:2 Seiber *Polka*

This is a cheeky, flirty polka, its clarity of texture and generally high register conveying the dance's small steps and feminine origins. Thinking 'polka dots', a fashionable pattern in the 1930s, will inspire the light, precise staccato needed to communicate the sense of fun; this is achieved with a bounce at the wrist, using the ends of the fingers with only a little weight. Carefully-crafted dynamic shapes will give the phrases direction to avoid heaviness, as will a refined balance between the hands, clear right-hand tone and light left-hand support. In order to maintain the character the tone shouldn't get too strong even at *forte* – again, the control here is dependent on a relaxed, bouncing wrist.

Imagination beyond the score might be needed to engage the listener. A slight holding-back of the tempo could be persuasive, perhaps in bar 9 on the return to the opening bars, with the grace note unobtrusive and tucked-in. This subtle temporal playfulness would also work elsewhere, such as into bar 13. The marked dynamics should be explored but the melodic line may be allowed more delicate shading (e.g. a decrescendo in bar 2 through the semiquavers), and there can be a little more impetus on the lower quavers of the bassoon-like left hand.

The last line is the trickiest but also the most captivating. Good awareness of left-hand notes and independence of the hands will be needed here to convey the free spirit of the end of the dance.

C:3 Sarah Watts *Strange Things Happen*

Secretive glances, crouching under windowsills and tiptoe footsteps are all here in what resembles a 1930s score to a silent film. It doesn't take much imagination to conjure up a storyline which will reflect the music's character.

It is in the subtle variety of articulation, dynamic and idiomatic jazz 'pushes' that the character resides. The suggested pizzicato bass sound has some resonance and length, so a longer crotchet staccato is more effective than something snatched, and couplet quavers need a light and short end. The detailed dynamic markings will convey the humorous suspense and surprises well – note particularly the *subito piano* in bars 7 and 23 and sudden *forte* in bar 9.

The suggested tempo is spot-on but a feel for the swung groove is crucial. For example, the quavers beginning bar 2 must be crotchet–quaver within a triplet, before a swung quaver chord anticipates beat 3. Small emphases on offbeat quavers will also give a jazz flavour, such as on the left-hand quaver A after the tie in bar 2, and the right-hand A♮ and A♭ in bar 7.

The laid-back feel must be underpinned by a strong sense of the pulse, a sense of theatre and a musical spontaneity which is only achieved with familiarity and good control. 'Shadow jumping' to the final Ds will help fingers to arrive on the notes with the confidence to shock the listener out of the seductive *piano* – a musical 'bursting of the balloon'.

C:4 Julian Anderson *Somewhere near Cluj*

This is a captivating, expressive song, its folk-style melody enhanced by a juxtaposition of the Mixolydian mode and G major. There is plenty to inspire and discuss: words that help shape the tune and enhance the phrasing, the use of alternative scales, and irregular phrase lengths.

The broad tempo demands subtle awareness of dynamic shape including feminine endings, and a progression towards the top of the phrase. The phrase markings may be considered in a vocal sense, rather than as articulation. Interpreting a group of slurred notes as a single word would enable a natural melodic line rather than a series of snatched breaths. The first three-bar phrase could be entirely legato but perhaps with the smallest of breaths between the second and third beats of the second bar. The phrase could grow dynamically to the D in bar 2, be lightly phrased off on the second beat, before growing again to the tenuto B and a soft final D.

As in all song-like pieces, good balance between the hands is essential, not least when the melody moves to the left hand in bar 18. Consistent, organized fingering will assist this and ensure a smooth movement of the hands both around the tune and between the accompanying 5ths/6ths.

The last two bars need space and time, the rest given its full length, and the cadence beautifully poised, the final sigh of this poignant story.

C:5 David Blackwell *Cat's Eyes*

Furtive and stalking, this cat only has its eyes on the prey and it gets its reward at the end. Think Pink Panther with evil designs and you'll grasp the tempo: not too fast and with an understanding of the essential swung groove, the semiquavers of the dotted-quaver groupings and the individual quavers all falling within this jazz feel.

An unfailing awareness of pulse and rhythm is absolutely essential; any clipping of beats (particularly the rests) will unsettle the padding progress of the predator, spoiling the effect. Rhythm work away from the piano will reap huge rewards, as will counting out loud (in time!) while playing. Light jazz 'pushes' will add to the feel; for instance, a tiny accent on the first quaver of bar 11 with a lighter G crotchet gives the right effect.

To enhance the character, articulation of the staccato needs to be light and short from the surface of the key with just a little weight behind the finger, and the overall sound should not be too heavy. Consideration of the *pianissimo* later on ought to encourage a fairly confident opening tone.

Dynamically shaping the melody will entice the prey into a false sense of beguiled security before the startled *forte* (bar 27), and a placed final chord (slightly later than expected) will enhance the drama of the cat's deathly pounce.

C:6 Stravinsky *Allegretto*

The collection's title *Les cinq doigts* (The Five Fingers) conveys the ease of playing the notes of this characterful piece, the difficulties lying purely in the imagination and storytelling, not in the articulation, notes or rhythm.

The pleading, persuasive melodic lines of the opening with its irregular phrase lengths speak perhaps of a manipulative young child who, not able to persuade through charm, resorts to stamping feet in a temper tantrum. A battle of wills ensues, the child eventually falling asleep. The piece clearly has its tale to tell.

The second (five-bar) phrase, perhaps the hardest to convey, should keep the tension and musical direction within a soft dynamic but must never be uniform, always rising and falling. The secret lies in a true legato, fingers and sound genuinely overlapping, with varying degrees of weight transferred from finger to finger to 'describe' the melodic line dynamically. The commas later on are there to define the phrases but not to cause a musical hiccup. Words will encourage a sense of flow and rise and fall, although the mind needs to prepare in advance for the 'stamp of the foot', which should be rhythmic, more detached and with a brighter tone. The right hand's *forte* needs to be maintained through the first note of the *piano* left-hand entry in bar 15 (also bar 21).

Though not marked, a gentle ritardando through the final quavers would give a peaceful end.

GRADE 3

Perhaps it is time to be a little more adventurous in the choice of pieces, now that exams are more of a familiar experience. Something of quite a different style might broaden the student's outlook, so it is well worth exploring the alternative pieces as well as the published selection.

A:1 C. P. E. Bach *Allegro in G*

This march has more charm than the image of heavy-footed soldiers might convey. It is part dance and part song, and its alternative scoring for woodwind suggests something far less robust and with greater poise.

The main technical challenges lie in the quick jumps between phrases (bars 4, 6, 12 etc.); while these mustn't delay the pulse they demand a change in dynamic, which is tricky when hands are moving quickly to position. To attain the control, thinking ahead is crucial: in bar 4 part of the action of playing the left-hand lower G should be immediate preparation of the upper G, the hand ready to play during the rest – similarly, the G in the right hand and preparation of the high B. An effective practice here is to shorten the crotchet G and move early; stop on the right hand's second B and check that the left hand is hovering over the right. Hands-together practice might consist of playing the final quaver of the bar a semiquaver early a few times.

The bassoon-like left hand needs a light, detached feel through the crotchets and the right-hand melody should be gently phrased with the articulative detail never extreme. There should be little difference between the two types of staccato marking – the 'wedge' shape perhaps just implying a quick jump. Semiquaver runs will respond to sensitive dynamic shaping; bars 5 to 6, for instance, need a small crescendo towards the top A with a stronger dynamic in the next two bars to anticipate the *forte*.

Clarity to the melodic line and awareness of balance will keep the piece alive and cheerful, trills should be melodic to avoid being intrusive or over-quick, and a little ritenuto at the end will enable the performer to finish with an elegant, white-gloved wave of the hand.

A:2 Haydn *German Dance in C*

It is in the stately and clearly defined rhythmic momentum of the opening that the character of this dance resides, and it opens up the opportunity for your student to investigate German dance tradition and culture. The Trio, with its somewhat comic grace notes, is rather tongue-in-cheek, and a wonderful contrast.

The notes present few problems; it is more the musical decision-making and control that provides the challenge. A feel for the light beats of each bar, the dance character and an enjoyment of the bold contrasts are needed to bring the piece to life. The positioning of the dynamic changes should be treated within the orchestral context from which they were taken, and not be played too abruptly. Elsewhere, for instance in bars 2, 6 and 24, the upbeats should be light and lead to the first beat of the bar, avoiding a literal interpretation of the phrasing which could easily lead to a disjointed melodic line. A smooth legato across the bar-line may be much more effective.

The Trio might benefit from a slight relaxation of tempo and mood. A nicely projected melodic line and light left-hand 3rds are needed initially, then the minim chords should be held for their full length. A slight lift at the bar-line will keep the charm. Thinking orchestrally, perhaps with the sound of a flute in mind, might promote subtle, yet playful grace notes.

The da capo allows the player to make a little more of the contrasts and to explore even greater musical shape and identity, as the dancers perhaps gain in confidence and authority.

A:3 S. Wesley *Vivace*

There is an inventive simplicity to this piece; its attractive folk-like melody is immediately appealing and tells its musical story without fuss. A priority is to find that 'perfect' tempo in which technical control permits subtlety of phrasing, articulation and balance while conveying the two-in-a-bar feel; the suggested metronome marking is a guide only.

Two tonal colours are needed: a bright, round-fingered neatness and dance-like quality to the melody with a gentler, harmonically supportive left hand. Plenty of separate practice might be needed to achieve the different timbres.

The right-hand phrasing provides a good starting-point for the articulation. The grace notes are lightly placed almost with the main note; the wrist 'drops' for the first note of the bar and the hand lightens as the bar progresses, 'dancing' with the phrasing. Two 'down' movements, one for each beat, should be avoided, as this will disjoint the longer melodic line;

to help here it would be perfectly acceptable to play the first five notes of the bar legato. The exception to this might be the middle section in which the couplet phrasing of the right-hand octave leaps gives a jaunty, carefree character.

The left hand should conscientiously hold the tonic, and its middle harmonic notes could be more legato than the phrasing indicates, though the rests in bar 3 must be heard and the lovely feminine ending in bar 4 highlighted. More harmonic support than is scored works well in bars 9–11, where slight over-holding of the first note of each quaver group will support the lyrical nature of this passage.

Finally, imaginative and song-like dynamic shading will enhance the four-bar phrases, giving them direction and personality. The dynamic contrasts at the end should be enjoyed – the final phrase the punchline to a hearty joke.

A:4 W. F. Bach *Allemande*

This is a delightful, bittersweet allemande with a memorable melody and beguiling charm. Subtlety of touch, phrasing and rhythmic nuance will unlock the character. The notes are not difficult and the suggested fingering works well, though alternatives can be explored if they are able to help hand movement and control.

A tempo of crotchet = *c.*72 is suitably gentle and unhurried, and should avoid the temptation of two strong accents in each bar. To maintain the graceful, dance character there need to be light, detached upbeats and a dynamic tracery of musically shaped phrases.

The first quaver, for instance, should be soft and slightly lifted, but not snatched, allowing for a placing of the first beat, a metaphorical bend of the knees, before lightening the second-beat and fourth-beat quavers within the first short phrase. This is repeated through the ascending phrase, the tone becoming slightly more insistent up to the beautifully expressive A on the third beat of bar 3. A tiny 'lean' into this gives it its poignancy before the phrase releases its tension.

The beginning of the middle section can be more demanding of attention; matching the articulation of the left-hand chords and melodic line will help the cohesiveness of the performance, as will grading the dynamic so that the *forte* can grow through the sequence without the sound becoming too robust or forthright. It will be important to keep the left hand a little lighter than the right to avoid too much sonority.

Bars 8–10 might be more legato in approach before the return, in bar 10, of the opening idea, which eventually meanders its way to an ingratiating bow.

A:5 Dittersdorf *English Dance in E flat*

This is a little gem – witty and tuneful with a hint of Classical opera. An appropriate choice of tempo is essential; a gentle two-in-a-bar at crotchet = *c.*85 works well and gives a casual, happy-go-lucky feel. Most of the piece falls comfortably under the fingers. Only bar 15 throws an awkward moment to the right hand, and here the B♭ mid-bar should be taken by the third finger so that the hand comes over the thumb and can join fluently into the 6th in bar 16.

Thinking in two-bar phrases with consistently light upbeats will enhance the charm. The initial turn on the first note may be technically challenging for young pianists and may be omitted if it can't be kept reliable, light and unobtrusive. The character lies then in the articulation, balance and creation of the appropriate sound-world; quavers should be mostly detached and the left hand kept lighter throughout than the right.

Subtle, detailed moments of dynamic shape and articulation will make a big difference. Growing through the right-hand 3rds to the first beat of bar 2, light 3rds in bar 3, a gentle lift and breath before the final quaver of bar 4, a decrescendo through the repeated chords in bars 9 and 10, and slightly accented melodic top notes to the semiquavers in bar 11 will all heighten the humour.

The final eight bars look deceptively easy and naive simplicity certainly works here, though again dynamic shading is needed, perhaps growing to the top F and then decreasing in volume towards the end. The 3rds and 6ths need a brighter top, since heavy notes below will make the sound too robust; instead imagine a 'whistling tune' with its gentle articulation and sunny ending.

A:6 L. Mozart *Menuet in A*

This is an attractive and charming piece with one of those melodies that sticks in the memory long after the practice session.

Playing musical detective can reveal more than just the notes. The piece is effectively in micro-sonata form: the 'first subject' is a four-bar phrase; the 'second subject' is in the dominant, cheekily contrasted rhythmically, followed by a mini two-bar coda; the 'development' (from the double barline) consists of four bars playing around with the two melodic patterns; the 'recapitulation' follows, with the second subject now in the tonic (bar 18). Explaining and revealing the structure in this way will help memorization, assist practice, and of course build up an awareness of Classical structure.

Subtle phrasing and articulation are needed to draw out the character in such dance-like movements, coupled with light upbeats and careful balancing of the hands. There should be no hint of robust tone in the left hand. The poetic, charming written-out appoggiaturas, such as the C♯ in bar 2 and the G♮ in bar 12, will benefit from a bit of time and placing, and to reflect the second subject there might be a change of colour in bar 5 and maybe an echo effect in bars 6–8. A *piano* contrast for the middle section works well, with perhaps a crescendo through to the restatement of the opening idea.

Smaller details can also be considered; a little lift before cadence points (e.g. the end of bar 9) will enhance the dance feel, and the student should aim for rhythmic detail which is natural and stable. This is particularly true through the triplets and semiquavers, which should not be rushed or distorted.

Not too much of a ritardando is needed at the end, just a relaxation into the wonderfully expressive final G♯ appoggiatura.

B:1 Chopin *Wiosna (Spring)*

One would think that spring was a time for rejoicing and happiness, but here the mood is distinctly melancholy. The poem that inspired the original song tells of a herdsman watching over his cattle. He contrasts the beauty of nature all around him with the sorrow that he carries in his heart – a typically Romantic muse.

The melody itself is folk-like and repetitive, just requiring a beautiful singing tone and expressive nuances to give it shape. Dynamics must be sensitively shaded, rising to little more than *mezzo-piano* in the outer sections. A brighter, more optimistic tone will help to emphasize the change of mood for the middle section when the mode changes from minor to major.

An important feature of the piece is the 'drone-like' pedal bass. It will be important to keep the left hand as relaxed as possible while it is anchored by the fifth finger, especially if it is to be played without pedal. The wrist should be allowed to rise and fall loosely as the hand moves towards and away from the thumb notes. It will be marginally easier if legato pedalling is employed, because once the pedal has been changed on the second beat the fifth finger can be released slightly early. For those with little experience of using the pedal, this piece provides an uncomplicated opportunity to develop the technique.

Whether the pedal is used or not, your student should aim for as smooth a flow as possible. A tiny ritenuto in the second half of bar 16 will mark the return to the minor, and *una corda* pedal will give a change of colour to the last four bars. The ending should sound unhurried as the scene fades from view.

B:2 T. Kirchner *Poco allegro*

The vitality and expressiveness of this attractive piece is bound to make it a popular choice. It will require agile fingers and sensitive use of dynamics, but above all confidence in moving about the keyboard.

There is a danger that the frequent jumps will break the phrasing and overstretch the beat, so plenty of slow practice with a steady pulse would be advisable at first. If the split octave in bar 10 seems to create a delay, it should first be practised with the notes struck together until it can be played comfortably in time. The technique of playing broken octaves (bars 12–14) may well be new to your student, and various preliminary steps can help towards ease of execution – for instance, playing only the thumb notes until they are memorized and the arm moves freely and is accurately positioned.

The ritenuto that begins in bar 6 must not be overdone or the music will come to a standstill before the *a tempo* is reached. However, the tempo is not fast; the leisurely crotchet = *c.*63 will be sufficient to meet the *Poco allegro* marking and to allow the expressive character of the piece to emerge. Ample dynamic marks are given which, if followed, will result in a colourful and shapely performance.

Pedal is not essential, but a few carefully placed touches will enhance the phrasing and make some of the shifts more comfortable. In bars 6–8, for example, the pedal can be fractionally depressed after the first beat and released on the second. This 'direct pedalling' allows a tiny breath between the phrases. Your student should enjoy the surprise in bar 14 when the music breaks off mid-phrase, and count the ensuing rests carefully before the final phrase.

B:3 Schubert *German Dance in A*

Dances are always popular, and the length of this delightful German Dance – just 16 bars – is an added attraction for the busy student. It is also simple in construction and lies comfortably under the hands.

In the melody line, the quavers should flow smoothly and evenly. Bars with crotchets, though, will create a pleasing lilt if beats 2 and 3 are staccato and a little lighter. For the waltz-like left hand, a slur from first beat to second will add a further spring to the rhythm. If pedal is used, a simple touch from first to second beat will highlight the slurs. It is possible to continue with the same pedalling throughout the dance, but the different rhythm and texture in bars 9–10 and 13–14 invites a change. Here the pedal could go down on the first beat and up on the third – or even sustain the whole bar. One could imagine the dancers swinging round energetically until resuming their more graceful steps to the quaver figures. If pedal is not possible (some students may not yet be ready to use it), a similar effect can be achieved by holding the left-hand E until releasing on the third beat.

As repeats are not expected, it would be a good idea to introduce more dynamic interest in the first half of the piece. For instance, the dynamic level at bar 5 might be slightly quieter (*mezzo-forte*), with a diminuendo to the end of the phrase. The suggested metronome mark of crotchet = *c.*144 gives the dance plenty of vitality, but it works well a little slower, too. As long as it sounds lively and rhythmic the dance will come to life.

B:4 Carroll *By Crystal Stream*

Generations of pianists, young and old, have enjoyed the music of Walter Carroll. Apart from their pedagogical value in helping to build technique, the pieces stimulate the imagination by describing pictures or poetic images, particularly of nature.

Coleridge's poem is about pixies, and the 'quiv'ring light' is that of the moon, so this immediately creates a scene of fantasy and mystery. The first feature to notice in this little gavotte is the rhythmic impetus created by the upbeat quaver chords of the first figure. They should spring lightly towards the crotchet chords of the first complete bar. These chords are marked as slurred staccato, and it is important that the two different types of staccato are clearly differentiated wherever they occur. The first phrase is then answered by a more flowing quaver figure.

In the piece's brief 26 bars, the composer employs many different effects through dynamics and articulation, and pedalling should be played as marked, even if some notes are staccato. Encourage your students to listen closely and they will hear that staccato with pedal has a special sound. Only a few fingerings are given, but in the left hand you might like to consider using 2/5 on the first two chords of the piece and 1/3 on the next. This works for all similar figures, even in bar 9 where the thumb will have to move forward for the F♯.

The phrasing is a regular 2 + 2 bars in length, until, beginning at the third beat of bar 12, a longer phrase, extended by a further two bars, rises to a climax as the reprise of the first theme (played *forte*) appears underneath – an exciting effect that should be relished by the performer.

B:5 C. Mayer *Study in C*

The idea of playing a study can seem boring to some students, so it is worthwhile asking a few questions during the first weeks of learning. What is the purpose of the study? If we gave it a descriptive title, what could it be? How can we make it as beautiful as possible? What is the shape or structure of the composition? Encourage your students to find their own answers.

The texture of the composition is a simple melody and accompaniment, so developing the ability to produce a lovely singing tone in the right hand while playing quietly with the left is going to be essential. However, the left-hand part will be found to have its own countermelody, which may be discreetly marked while keeping the repeated offbeat notes (G for the first six bars) very subdued.

The structure of a piece is always important, and it is an area of performance that is often overlooked. Realizing that the principal theme is played three times – bars 1–4, 5–8 and 13–16, with more elaboration added each time – will greatly help your students achieve a meaningful interpretation. Careful observation of the dynamics will also help to give shape. In bars 9–12 a new tune appears, and every effort should be made to play the upper notes as legato as possible, especially the minims. In bar 9, however, the left hand begins as if imitating the main theme again, so that needs to be given a little more prominence. The climax of the piece is in bar 11 and, as it subsides in bar 12, a *poco ritenuto* could be used to herald the return of the main theme, now lavishly decorated.

B:6 Swinstead *In the Bay*

The flowing, undulating lines of this descriptive piece conjure up images of a boat sailing through the gentle waves of a sunlit bay. The picture may be serene, but this piece is not for the faint-hearted.

Agility and the ability to negotiate some awkward hand-shifts will be essential for a successful performance. It would be sensible to tackle some of the trickiest corners first so that the fingering becomes automatic, for instance, the right-hand passage from the second beat of bar 2 to the first beat of bar 4. Here the fingering could start with finger 3 on B, then 1-2-3-5-4-1-5-3, ending with thumb on G. Once this feels easy, your student should find the whole phrase flows smoothly and evenly from the beginning. Just employ a gentle crescendo and diminuendo to follow the arc of the phrase. There is a similar pattern from the second beat of bar 6 to the first of bar 8, but with a slightly altered ending. The next two phrases employ a fingering sequence, the pivotal point being the placing of the thumb on the first note in bars 10 and 14.

Pedal, which is essential for texture and colour, can be employed in many places other than where marked in the score. However, it needs to be avoided where the left hand has scalic figures, such as in bars 18, 20 and 21.

Special attention should be paid to the passage beginning in bar 25 which requires an accelerando. It is as though a playful breeze catches the sails of the boat, making it skim through the waves. The *a tempo* at bar 32 shouldn't be overlooked, and from here to the end the *una corda* pedal will help to create the impression of the boat disappearing beyond the horizon.

C:1 Sullivan *The Policeman's Song*

Humour must be at the heart of any performance of this G & S classic from *The Pirates of Penzance*. Watching the DVD or, better still, going to a live performance would pay dividends. Gilbert and Sullivan were the masters of this type of comic song and in this witty arrangement a good starting point would be to locate the orchestral phrases, the solo vocal line and the brief refrains sung by the chorus of policemen.

The vocal phrases begin just before bar 5 and finish in bar 24. Reliable keyboard geography is required, as a span of four-and-a-half octaves needs to be negotiated. Singing is the best way to cultivate a natural sense of phrasing and this song requires a particularly pliable, flexible approach.

The melody, starting in the bass register at the upbeat into bar 5, wants to have a warm, weighted legato touch but it should be borne in mind that *pesante* does not imply a slower speed. The brief chorus inserts, first appearing in bar 6, should humorously and sharply interrupt the ponderous flow of the policeman's delivery.

The numerous expressive markings are necessary to reflect the operatic style. An intake of breath before, and holding back on, the upbeat quavers into bar 13 is required by the tenuto marking. The quaver upbeats in the bars that follow must not be laboured in case the musical flow becomes compromised. However, the chord at bar 20 could very slowly arpeggiate upwards, with each note fully sustained. A touch of direct pedalling would give this further resonance.

In the original version the first and last four bars are orchestral, conveyed here by the varied articulation. The *poco accel.* and *scherzando* in the postlude give a brief moment of comic delight before order is restored in the slow and grandiose final two bars.

C:2 Manfred Schmitz *Zur Sonnenuntergangsstunde (At Sunset)*

This wonderfully evocative, almost hypnotic composition will entrance those students with imagination and sensitivity. Schmitz's footnotes are particularly enticing and suggest that a performance would benefit from memorization, although this is not expected in the exam. The music has close to a timeless feel and the playing should be devoid of accentuation – especially on the semibreves at the beginning of each bar. In fact, the sound-world should be almost translucent. Dynamic changes are all fairly subtle, even the *mezzo-forte* in bar 5 (the loudest level in the piece), but within this limited resource some variation of colour is still achievable.

Although it is usual to count 6/4 in dotted minims, here it is necessary to feel the tempo in crotchets as indicated by the metronome mark. Phrasing, however, needs to be forward-flowing and flexible, and this will require a convincing sense of rubato from your student. The four-note arabesque-like figure that starts the piece and introduces each phrase should have a little elasticity, especially in order to coax us into the *a tempo* which occurs after each ritardando. The left hand needs fluidity and ease when crossing over the right. Physical appearance when playing this piece will also be important because awkward mannerisms could detract from the total effect. An intuitive player will savour the pedalling which is straightforward and adds atmosphere. Indeed, it is impossible to perform this music convincingly without pedal and this might be a consideration when deciding which piece to play from the list.

The ritardandos should not be started too early as this will affect the flow, particularly at the end where the quavers are like wisps of cloud rising into infinity. The overall effect should leave listeners mesmerized, as if they are contemplating the mysterious glow that is cast at sunset.

C:3 Dave Stapleton *Blue Sky Blues*

This understated blues is full of interesting and unusual chords. The insistent swung rhythms need to be supported by confident, sustained harmonies. Looking at the harmonic structure and what makes this sound slightly unfamiliar might be a good starting-point. It would be worth highlighting the dissonances which occur throughout and also the use of augmented and diminished intervals that can be found for example in bars 5–7. Some useful aural and theoretical work could be integrated here if it can be made fun and not overly academic.

A strict, consistent beat should underpin the swung quavers, and the rests and tied notes must be meticulously timed. There might be a temptation to anticipate the second-beat chord in bar 8 and also to clip the tied-quaver-to-minim chords in bars 12–14 and 16, so particular care will be needed here. Dynamics are clear and the crescendos indicated will give shape and direction to the rising patterns. The crisp, slightly accented final bar must be played *tempo giusto*. As the title perhaps suggests, this needs to have an easy-going and laid-back groove.

The teacher is usually on to a winner with this style of music, as it should appeal to a wide range of students. Rhythm and counting could be found particularly challenging, however, and embracing the rhythmic as well as harmonic complexities of the music will need patience. Precision should be insisted upon from the outset but some imaginative rhythmic games could make the whole process fun. Students should also listen to some standard and contemporary blues in order to engage fully with the idiom.

C:4 Bartók *Jest*

A familiar teasing game that children love to play is beautifully encapsulated in this little gem, which comes from Bartók's collection *For Children*.

The right-hand figuration in bars 5–8, for instance, is reminiscent of a mimicking children's rhyme. The jest or joke of the title is to be found in the subdued rallentando of bars 12–13, 28–9 and 42–5, also in bars 32 and 46 which contain a pensive pause. With their unexpected harmonic shifts they create an air of suspense and mystery, and students can enjoy deciding what the joke is going to be. These bars are immediately followed by peals of jovial laughter.

The rhythms and notes are reasonably straightforward but legato against staccato touch will need due consideration, especially in bars 21–4 and 35–8. The left-hand quavers in bars 17–24, 33–43 and 49–52 need to be very even, for which a gentle rotating movement of the wrist will help. The crossing of hands in the last three bars requires anticipation and the right hand should have a crisp, marcato attack free from any tension.

A brisk tempo is ideal but the speed must allow the right-hand staccato quavers to be articulated clearly. It is important that the *a tempo* bars are exact, so a useful initial exercise would be to omit, or imagine but not play, the rallentando bars. The pacing of these bars is crucial and imagination will also be required. Interestingly the first direction is only for a *poco rall.* The rallentando of each jest is slightly more drawn out than the last. The final five bars are an uncontrollable explosion of laughter which erupts into a *fortissimo* finish.

C:5 Brian Chapple *Blues*

Judging just the right speed is the key here – a little too slow and the left-hand crotchets feel laboured, but too fast and the triplets and dotted rhythms appear rushed. Mr Chapple suggests an appropriate metronome mark which helps to convey the laid-back blues style while giving the music a sense of forward direction.

Throughout the piece the left hand wants to have a grounded, slightly weighted feel (hence the tenuto marks) but should not be accented. In bars 12, 14 and 15 both hands play crotchets with tenuto staccato markings, and here the blend and balance should be carefully considered. The dotted rhythms should be played with a triplet swing throughout as indicated at the top of the score, including the dotted-quaver rest/semiquaver note at bars 12 and 14.

Initially the dynamics should be quite mellow; not bland but slightly understated and smoky. The upbeat into bar 13 is a repetition of the previous phrase and the tonal colour here should have more intensity, continuing to grow to the climax at bar 17. The wide spacing between the hands and the *forte* accents should be savoured, especially after the impact of the minim rest. After the next minim rest, in bar 19, a sonorous warm tone is again required and this would be enhanced by some pedal. However, it is important that the rhythm is kept really taut until the end. The grace notes which appear throughout the piece should be relaxed and not clipped.

Encouraging students to listen to examples of trad. jazz or famous blues singers such as Billie Holiday would certainly get them into the groove!

C:6 Gillock *The Juggler*

This piece, which will appeal to a great many students, is a real winner. A circus atmosphere must prevail, and the choice of an appropriate tempo is crucial in enabling the *scherzando* character to be conveyed. The music seems to swivel precariously, almost as if the juggler is about to topple but never actually does. A successful performance would be possible at a number of different speeds, but for this grade, crotchet = c.96 would be a sensible choice.

To this end it is important that the positioning of the right hand is carefully judged in order to ensure that the fingers fully cover the black notes. To help your students with this, you could suggest they first practise playing the semiquavers as scrunched-up chords.

The music has humour and cheerfulness in abundance, and the need to convey the wide range of dynamics and articulation cannot be overemphasized. The role of the right hand seems to be to keep the audience enthralled with skilful manoeuvres and antics while the left hand is responsible for the precisely timed juggling of balls. The left hand should be light and buoyant and a slight rotation of the wrist will help prevent any tension (especially in smaller hands), whereas deft, nimble finger-work is needed in the right hand. During bars 19–30 there is a sense of pausing to reflect or to create suspense, but the tempo here must not slacken even for a moment, apart from the carefully timed *rit.* which leads us back to yet more clowning.

The last four bars possibly suggest the juggler exiting the stage on tiptoe, and these bars must be light, soft and preferably *a tempo*.

GRADE 4

Many of the List B pieces will now benefit from some pedal, but if you feel that your student is not quite ready, don't forget that further options are available on the alternative list. The musical personality of students often becomes more firmly established at this stage and they can play to their strengths, making the most of contrasts in tempo and mood.

A:1 Anon. *March in E flat*

To capture the character of this lively march one has only to imagine a colourful scene at court. An orchestra with trumpets and drums accompanies a procession of lords and ladies in all their finery.

The suggested metronome mark of minim = *c.*66 provides a suitably brisk tempo, which may be felt as two-in-a-bar to avoid sounding too square. Crotchets, especially those in the left hand, will sound best if they are detached. The mix of quavers with slurs and those without provides scope for contrasting a smooth legato touch with a more brilliant finger action. Many phrases have repeated notes, and care should be taken to keep them light and buoyant. It is only rarely that the same notes within a group are given equal tone.

There are just a few dynamic marks given, showing the overall structure of the piece. However, the shape of the phrasing suggests gradations of tone within that framework. For instance, the first phrase rises to the first beat of bar 2 and gradually falls away to its conclusion in bar 4. The next two bars could be *forte* followed by two quieter bars, and there is an opportunity for echo effects later. There are no hard and fast rules, and it will be fun for your student to decide what dynamics to use. The descending left-hand notes of the cadences at the end of each section should ideally be tapered, though.

The few trills are not unduly fast and are clearly annotated in the score, as are all necessary fingerings. Once comfortably secure, this is a piece that will give pleasure to both player and listener alike.

A:2 A. E. Müller *Scherzo in F*

The spirited, colourful character of this piece makes it a joy to play. There are some challenges, but its infectious good humour encourages one to play it over and over – not a bad thing if it is practised carefully!

As the footnote suggests, articulation in bar 5 (and similar) could be staccato in order to match bar 1. In bars 27–33 the curved lines indicate legato so it is better to play that passage without breaking at the bar-lines. While your student is at the stage of separate-hand practice, fingering should be a priority. For instance, in bar 6 the exact placing of finger 2 on F in the rising arpeggio is crucial, and it would be worthwhile marking thumb on A in bars 47 and 71 so that the following notes flow safely. Some players might prefer to use third finger on the C in bars 48 and 72.

Once hands are together, extra care will be needed when one hand has a different articulation to the other. In bars 9–10 and 13–14, for example, the left hand has slurs while the right plays staccato, and in the passage from bar 51 to bar 56 there are overlapping tied notes and slurs to be negotiated. Pedal is not essential, but occasional touches will add variety and provide technical security. It could be held through bar 6, and in bar 20 a simple direct pedal will mark the slur. Another quick pedal (from first to second beat) in bars 55 and 56 will help to sustain the right-hand slurs there.

Dynamic marks are generous, and if these are employed along with nuances that follow the shape of the phrasing a lively and attractive performance should result.

A:3 D. Scarlatti *Sonata in G minor*

With its melancholy mood and flowing style, this is a piece that will appeal to the thoughtful student who can produce good tone and expressive phrasing.

The structure is straightforward. Two closely related themes are repeated several times with subtle alterations, shifting from the tonic G minor to the relative major and back again. It is full of sighing suspensions and gentle ornaments, and the suggested metronome mark (crotchet = *c.*44) allows the music an unhurried flow.

A warm singing tone will be needed for both hands, and it would be helpful to imagine the piece played either by violin and cello, or by wind instruments. The main theme is in the treble, but the bass line also needs shaping and to be given the sort of attention that would be lavished on it by a solo instrument. Wherever notes are repeated (e.g. right hand, bars 1 and 4; left hand, bars 4 and 5) they must be as legato as possible. The finger should remain in the key, just easing upwards sufficiently to allow the second note to be replayed. Use of sustaining pedal is not advisable for fear of smudging detail.

Ornaments are all played on the beat and are clearly annotated in the score. The decorative figures in bars 11 and 12 should be light and gently shaped – this passage is perhaps the heart of the piece, its falling sequences expressing great tenderness. Overall, the dynamic range is quite narrow and the suggested dynamic marks do not exceed *mezzo-forte*. The final phrase, which sounds like a refrain, might be effective with *una corda* pedal, and a *poco ritenuto* in the last bar will bring this beautiful piece to a calm conclusion.

A:4 Diabelli *Moderato cantabile*

It is never too early for students to begin to grasp structure in music. Understanding in the simplest of terms that a piece may have a first tune (A), a second, contrasting melody (B), and then a return of the first (A) will help even the most elementary student to play with more musical understanding. By Grade 4 it could be time to learn about sonata form.

This Diabelli movement would be a perfect place to start as it contains in miniature everything that can be found in larger-scale works. The four-bar first subject is made up of expressive appoggiaturas or suspensions that must be lovingly shaped. This is followed by a bridge passage which serves to modulate to the dominant (C major) for the second subject. Beginning in bar 8, this tune is more spiky and athletic in character, ending with a rising semiquaver scale and the traditional exposition repeat sign. (Ignore this in the exam!)

The development begins with a version of the first subject, initially in G minor then passing through C minor. This passage is the emotional heart of the movement, so encourage your student to enjoy the pain and stresses as the music gradually builds in volume only to arrive happily in C major again (bar 20). A short cadenza-like passage (bars 22–4) leads back to the home key of F major and the recapitulation. All passion spent, the first subject appears reassuringly again exactly as before, but the bridge passage changes a little so that the second subject may appear in the home key. The movement is then rounded off with a triumphant three-bar coda.

A:5 J. N. Hummel *Minuetto in F*

The gracefulness and elegance of this minuet are very appealing. It is full of ideas, and although it is from a later date than many of Mozart's minuets, there are similarities that are unmistakable.

The score already contains a great deal of information by way of articulation and dynamics to guide the pianist towards a stylish performance, and this should all be carefully noted. A metronome mark of crotchet = *c.*100 will give a stately lilt to the dance, but it is better felt as one-in-a-bar with a lift to the third beats. Dynamics should not be too extreme, and many of the hairpin diminuendo marks (bar 1 etc.) merely indicate the shape of slurs. The quaver rest that appears after the double bar-line at bar 8 is unintentional, and the triplet upbeat of the following section should not be delayed.

The contrasting Trio is contrapuntal in nature, and hands are of equal importance as one follows the other in quiet conversation. The character is more plaintive, too, especially in the chromatic figures of the bars marked *poco rinf. ed espress.*, and smooth flowing legato lines will give contrast to the Minuetto.

Pedal can be employed to help make the cadences at the end of each section more legato. Just a touch might help on the first beat of bar 8 and on the last bar of the Minuetto. In the Trio pedal may be used for the last two bars of each section, changing on each bass note and releasing on the low D.

In the exam, repeats should not be played except for the da capo return of the Minuetto.

A:6 L. Mozart *Allegro in G*

One can imagine the four-year-old Mozart sitting at the harpsichord playing this delightful Allegro that father Leopold had just written for him. It is a piece that will certainly appeal to the student who enjoys lively music.

A crisp finger touch should be employed for the right-hand semiquavers, and lightly detached quavers for the left. However, in bars 11–12 and 31–2 a smooth legato line of left-hand quavers will give melodic support to the offbeat chords above and add variety to the texture. This can be followed by a slur on the first two quavers of bars 13 and 33 to mark the approach to the cadences.

The right hand has most of the technical demands, but there are a few bars where the left has to be as agile. It would be worthwhile preparing bars 20–23 and 34–7 in advance. The given fingering for the demisemiquavers in bars 22 and 36 suggests that the fifth finger lands on the F♯dotted crotchet. While this is perfectly feasible, beginning with the second finger followed by the thumb will allow the stronger fourth finger to arrive on F♯.

The appoggiaturas follow the basic rules of taking either half the value of the principal note (e.g. bar 4) or two-thirds (bar 14). It would be stylish to add an appoggiatura to the final bar, too. Although there were probably no dynamics in the original score, the piece will need them when played on the modern piano. If the score is free from editorial markings, encourage your student to decide what dynamics will work and to write them in.

A metronome speed of dotted crotchet = *c*.52 will bring sparkle without danger!

B:1 Alwyn *The Sun is Setting*

The descriptive features of this evocative piece are most alluring and will really stimulate the imagination of a receptive and sensitive student.

A beautiful cantabile legato touch is necessary to help shape the simple folk-like phrases, and to give warmth and aid fluency the legato pedalling is essential. However, it is crucial to listen to its effect rather than simply follow the pedal markings, particularly if a piano is unfamiliar and the acoustic different. Small adjustments might be needed especially when the melodic line is in the bass or middle register. For example, between bars 38 and 45 the cantabile melody could easily become blurred. In bars 46–7 and 48–9 the pedal change is marked at the beginning of the second bar, but a swift change on the last quaver before the bar-line, as well as where indicated, might produce a clearer result.

Alwyn was a professional flautist as well as a composer and one could imagine the opening 37 bars of the right hand being played by a flute. The piece needs a wide tonal palette and thinking of this instrumentally will help to evoke different colours. For example, the melody in the tenor register in bars 38–45 would be ideal for the cello; imagining this would help give the music a nostalgic glow. There might be a clarinet (or, as the footnote suggests, a violin) in bars 46–53 (first quaver), with the flute returning to play the rising whole-tone scalic figures in bars 53–9.

The harmonic writing creates an atmospheric mood. In bars 16–17 the chromatic descending 3rds suggest the sun slipping behind the clouds, casting eerie shadows. The wonderfully unexpected and magical chord in bars 60–61 which shrouds the music in mystery again is evocative of the Impressionist school. However, the reassuring concord finishes the piece with a note of optimism.

B:2 Trad. Latvian, arr. Garūta *Silta, jauka istabiņa (The Warm and Pleasant Room)*

Latvian folksongs – as with all other folksongs – are diverse in their character, and the warmth that comes from this arrangement is particularly emotive. One senses a great comfort-blanket of feeling in a cosy snug room with a Latvian winter raging outside.

The piece gives an opportunity to develop legato, cantabile tone and part-playing – and to deal with shifting metres and possibly rubato. The *amoroso* marking certainly suggests that this music should be played with affection and tonal resonance. The opening two bars are an introduction. The folk tune appears in the right hand in bars 3–10 and then in the left hand in bars 11–18b (omitting the first-time bar for exam purposes). Singing the melody through will help to develop a natural sense of phrasing. The movement is mostly stepwise with a few descending 3rds which makes the melody eminently singable, even for the most reluctant student! The counter-theme is also very melodious, and gives the texture an attractive duet-like quality. Both parts should flow and passages where the time signature alternates between 2 and 3 might be felt in quintuple metre. In bars 4–5 the countermelody overlaps the main melody, thus maintaining fluidity of the line. Phrase contours are given emphasis by the hairpins but the loudest point should not exceed *mezzo-forte*. The tone however wants always to have a singing quality, even at *pianissimo* level.

Finally, some judicious pedalling is advisable but only once good legato control has been mastered in both hands. Attentive listening will be essential in order to avoid any blurring of the lines.

B:3 Grieg *Alvedans (Dance of the Elves)*

An insistent beat, crisp articulation and a lively tempo will evoke this mischievous dance. The minor key here gives these elves a somewhat dark and menacing quality. Good keyboard geography and supple wrists are needed throughout.

It should be in a steady one-in-a-bar, with a securely anchored pulse; rushing would adversely affect stability and co-ordination. Technical demands should be considered first, and voicing, balancing and co-ordinating the staccato chords will require slow practice. It is worth taking time to decide which notes should have prominence and usually this will be associated with melodic movement. For example, from the right hand's

B-B-C-B-B and left hand's E-E-C-E-E in bars 1–2 there emerges a little motif which will become more common. Skilful voicing is also needed in the soft, thicker-textured chords in bars 68–70, where this motif is slightly extended. The embellishments in the last two bars may be played either on or before the beat.

The quavers in bars 3–4 require a pliable lateral wrist movement, especially in bar 4 where an octave is spanned. To prevent the wrist becoming tense, rotary movement is necessary at various points, such as in bars 7–8, 15–16 and 19–20. The use of pedal should be minimal so that the *sempre staccato* effect is maintained. However, the few bars where pedal is indicated give a little respite to the driving percussive nature of the music.

This highly descriptive piece will need plenty of imagination to convey the magical, almost frenzied scene. Communicating the wide dynamic range (*ppp–f*/*fz*) is essential. In general a light, incisive and agile touch is required, as if conveying spells being scattered while the elves dance their intoxicating, slightly demonic steps.

B:4 S. Heller *Con moto, scherzando*

This attractive piece is in fact a study in agility, dexterity and articulation. The focus for technical development is the semiquavers: two figurations dominate (those beginning in bars 1 and 9), and a third patterning is found at bars 27–8. The four semiquavers should be practised slowly, finishing on the following beat. Varying the rhythm and articulation will also stimulate fluency and evenness.

A still hand-position is required for the first group (i.e. from bar 1), and the implied accent on the first semiquaver provides the impetus for the fingers to ripple over the notes that follow. In the second group the left hand's scale-like figure resolves onto the F♯ quaver played in the right hand. A slight rotary movement here will dissuade any possible wrist tension. Passing the notes from one hand to the other requires particular attention and control. In the third group hand-positioning needs to be carefully anticipated. One could imagine these shimmering semiquavers as a cascading waterfall. Playing the semiquaver groups as block chords would help to secure this, but ultimately there needs to be fluid crossing of the hands with the notes dancing lightly.

The piece is otherwise straightforward, but the student should guard against unnecessary accents, e.g. on the third beat of bar 1 and the second beat of bar 4. Meticulous rhythmic preparation is needed to avoid miscounting – for example in bar 4, on minims (bar 17, beats 2–3), and especially in bars 29–30.

The essential musical character is light-hearted and playful. A gentle one-in-a-bar will give buoyancy and momentum. However, the speed is ultimately determined by the ability to play the semiquavers with clarity. The dynamics need to be vivid, with the sudden changes noted, and close attention paid to the accents and *sforzando* markings.

B:5 Merkel *The Merry Huntsman*

This cheerful jaunty piece is reminiscent of 'Jägerliedchen' from Schumann's *Album für die Jugend* and poses few technical demands or rhythmic challenges. Despite the printed tempo marking, a more suitable tempo for Grade 4 will be closer to crotchet = 100.

The phrases are clearly defined with the melody played initially in octaves, in bars 1–2, alternating with a characteristic 'horn-call' motif in bars 3–4. The octaves require a firm, cantabile quality and the last three notes of the phrase should be tapered. Articulation and dynamic marks must be followed in bars 2–3 particularly and at similar points in order to give a buoyant lilt and provide suitable contrast.

The echo in bars 20–21 should be quite different in dynamic from what has gone before, but the touch must still be firm in the softer playing; coordination could be problematic if approached in an overly tentative way. At this point younger players especially might be tempted to shuffle up the stool, but this should be discouraged. The torso and arms move around to reach higher up the keyboard but the sitting position should remain unaltered. One might imagine the body as the trunk of a tree (rooted to the piano stool) with the arms as branches reaching to meet the top notes.

The *sforzando* chords in bars 28 and 29 could be very slightly detached for emphasis but still accentuated. In contrast to this the right hand in bars 33–7 should begin delicately with a gently rotating wrist movement, and from the second half of bar 35 more tonal brilliance will be needed.

The performance should leave the listener with a feeling of lilting good humour.

B:6 Hugo Reinhold *Melancolie*

This hauntingly beautiful piece will really suit a sensitive student. The performance requires an instinctive response to the expressive lyrical lines, with pliable and flexible phrasing. It offers a good opportunity to discuss or even introduce rubato.

A stately tempo, without any sense of dragging can be achieved with a metronome speed of crotchet = *c.*80. The overlapping phrases are divided between the hands and there should be a natural flow into the middle of the phrase, before dying away, letting the next phrase take over. As the pitch rises the expression intensifies. The repeated note over the bar-line, occurring first over bars 2–3 and 4–5, then reverting to the left hand, is an expressive device which, as indicated, needs to taper on its descent.

The tone wants to be sonorous and legato throughout. A rich, velvety 'string sound' could be imagined and judicious pedalling is recommended, especially in the last four bars. If the pedal is used elsewhere, great care should be taken not to blur the melodic lines or harmonies.

Each phrase should naturally ebb and flow with the quavers having a little more forward impetus, but without any feeling of rushing. The climax of the piece arrives at bar 24, but emotion has been building from bar 17 and, with the *poco accel.*, the drama surges with intensity. No ritardando or *a tempo* is written in bars 24–5 but this is surely implied. The passion of the music is maintained after bar 25 and reinforced in bar 29 before the mood gradually subsides. Small hands might struggle with legato control in the final descending chords so pedal would aid fluency.

C:1 Emmanuel Oriol *Ne tirez pas sur le pianiste! (Don't Shoot the Pianist)*

The clever title and Chaplinesque character will undoubtedly make this piece a popular choice. It is in a lively ragtime style but with that comes the excitement (and perils!) of a leaping left hand; it must jump to its notes unsupervised, since the focus of attention is primarily on the witty melody.

To this end it is crucial to begin practising with the left hand, developing a physical memory for the bass line and chords. Consistent fingering is needed so that the measured distance is the same each time it is played; the technique should be relaxed, dropping with a pliant arm and wrist on the bass notes to give them some warmth and length, with a lightening of the hand for the chord, played as if on the way back down for the next bass note. When there are two consecutive single notes after the left-hand pattern changes (bar 6) they can be lightly detached, leading towards the next bar. Once the accompaniment can almost be played with eyes closed the hands may be put together.

The right hand is fairly straightforward musically though there is scope for a variety of articulation. For example, a slightly detached feel to some of the semiquavers would emphasize the personality. There are next to no dynamics early on in the piece, but professional pianists would instinctively put in a range of dynamic contrast and shading to enhance the performance.

Tempo choice will be paramount to success, and your students should aim for a tempo within which they can achieve control, accuracy and a subtlety of shape, perhaps in the region of crotchet = 88. There is no need to put oneself in front of the firing squad here.

C:2 Federico Ruiz *La peruanita (The Little Peruvian Girl)*

This wonderful piece is a story in two halves: the opening is a melancholy folksong perhaps, vocal in character, but troubles are soon left behind, and this little Peruvian girl dances her way back home.

The opening melody needs a true legato; adjacent notes might be overlapped slightly with the fingers to blend the line, particularly at first, and with a dynamic rise and fall throughout. Putting words to the tune will help this, particularly if they illustrate the softer ending of the first phrase and the more positive end of the second. Bars 10 and 12 need good control so that the harmonic E is not intrusive – similarly with the C in bars 14 and 15.

A subtle lift should be made before the conflicting D♮ in bar 17, which could sound like a mistake unless it is cheekily communicated. A musical 'raising of the eyebrow' is appropriate here, with a little time taken over the tenuto notes. The *non legato* right hand needs control and subtlety; a slightly higher wrist will help keep it light as will more focus to the top of the hand (avoiding heavy thumbs).

The left hand works well if the detail is followed, namely legato where marked and lightly detached elsewhere. The challenge is to keep the chords much lighter than the bass notes to avoid a heavy-footed second and third beat; the chords should have a slightly higher wrist and a hint of hand weight without too much energy in the fingers. The hand will travel easily to its notes once the physical memory is well-ingrained.

Just a little ritardando is needed at the end, enough to allow a flirtatious, unhurried *pianissimo* arpeggio in the right hand as the girl happily skips away.

C:3 Poul Ruders *Swinging Bells*

If ever there were an excuse to explore the hidden art of campanology this is it. Ringing the changes, method ringing and even 'Plain Bob Minor' are all worth investigating, as are the many beautiful recordings of some of the world's famous peals of bells.

The bells here are admittedly smaller than traditional church bells due to their high register but the pianistic effects called for by the score are mesmerizing and atmospheric. There is actually nothing hard about this piece providing that the performer has a good sense of pulse and can count up to seven; it is a gift in terms of note learning. It needs, however, some careful co-ordination of the hands and an ear for balance to create a successful sound-world. The rhythmic complexity and feel for the changing time signatures can easily be internalized away from the piano with some clapping or rhythmic games/duets.

Holding the harmonic left hand is crucial to the overall resonance, providing a pianistic echo effect, which can be enjoyed and savoured on the longer chords but shouldn't be too loud or bell-like by itself. Instead the brighter tone is better saved for the right-hand notes, which need to be played with energy and a slight bounce from just above the key surface.

All the markings should be treated within context – nothing too severe or accented on the G♯s or top Es, for instance. Above all, hands must be absolutely together, the swinging bells co-ordinated with absolute precision.

The final pedal marking provides a fabulous depth and sonority for the hitherto unheard 'tenor' bell. The pedal must go down just before the essential release of the chord so that it can be heard darkly in the harmonic echo and decay of the upper notes.

C:4 Valerie Capers *Billie's Song*

It's well after midnight, the band has left, and the nightclub singer begins one final, soulful love-song at the piano. This is not just another pastiche jazz-style piece but music that is wholly idiomatic and convincing, with sumptuous harmonies and an elegantly turned melody.

The two-in-a-bar marking is important to the flow and pedalling is essential to the line and atmosphere. It can be simply managed, needing only a gentle change after each first-beat harmony and, occasionally, mid-bar (bars 16–18).

The right hand's 'song' should be projected while underlying harmonies are kept gentle yet supportive. Practising top line and harmonies as a duet will establish the balance needed before the physical control is developed to achieve the same effect within one hand; this comes from a faster movement into the keys from the fingers carrying the tune. One effective strategy is to depress the accompanying notes slightly and, without releasing, play a projected top note until this feels comfortable; then to allow the lower notes to play (without lifting first), developing a feel for the independence. The moving accompaniment shouldn't interfere with held melodic notes, e.g. F♯–F♮ in bar 4.

A natural pliancy and improvisatory rubato will give the song more of a narrative, and a slight adjustment to the published fingering will better link the melody across the bar-line. In bar 1, for example, use a 3 instead of a 4 on the A, and in bar 3, use third finger on G.

The *mezzo-forte* dynamic needs care – too light and the music will sound tentative, too heavy and it will lose its persuasive soul. It needs to be warm, gently and dynamically shaped within this context, with a dreamy 'lights-out' final bar.

C:5 Kabalevsky *Dance*

This quirky, comic-like circus dance is a gift for an outgoing, confident student, though it plays its cheeky tricks on both the audience and the performer. Since it is in ABA form there are not too many bars to learn, but some tricky moments need to be overcome.

Work should begin with the middle section, bars 24 to 44, as this may be where some promising performances fall apart. The hands need to find their notes with flawless confidence and well ahead of time. As practice the left hand's grace note can be played simultaneously with the first right-hand chord in each bar, the final chord of the bar played separately – making sure that the hands move positively to the next chord immediately on the release of the previous one. The co-ordination of the pedal might also prove a little uneasy here but the passage can work without pedal, more physical overlap of the sound giving a similar effect.

The fingering should be reassessed to make sure it works well for the individual. The secret to a jokey opening is avoiding an accent on the upbeat semiquavers, ensuring a buoyant bounce on the first beat; 4-3-5 might encourage this. Bars 9 to 16 might use a strict chromatic-scale fingering rather than any less familiar alternatives.

The piece relies on a strong contrast of articulation, from the very short staccato of jumping and mocking dance steps to a 'swaying on the feet' over-legato in the semiquavers. The articulation should always be incorporated into the slow practice.

Dynamic shaping will naturally be needed throughout but particular attention should be given to the *forte* contrast in the middle section and the diminuendo at the end as the clowns leave the stage on tiptoe.

C:6 Carl Vine *Semplice*

There is a minimalist, film-music feel to this haunting, beautiful piece; a loving couple part for the final time amid tears, their eyes full of sadness.

The piece is vocal and improvisatory in nature, most of it consisting of sad, appealing phrases sung in one breath. The most intense part of the phrase is sometimes the first, which gradually dies away, as in the opening, but at other times the phrase grows to the middle or end. Feel the phrases across two bars, but notice the beautiful extended four-bar phrase, bars 13 to 16, before the return of the opening.

A clearly projected and dynamically shaded melodic line is crucial throughout, with a natural, musical pliancy and smooth true legato. A technically drilled approach to the fingers is not suitable here; instead the melody needs sensitivity of touch from the surface of the keys. It would be easy to spoil the mood with abrupt, disjointed pedal. Your student need have no embarrassment about the slightly clouded harmonic feel that would be created by a gentle and slow pedal lift, though they must ensure that there is space for the rest.

Little is written in terms of dynamics but a musically engaging performance still should have contrast, perhaps making a diminuendo to *pianissimo* in bars 7–8, and playing the middle section a more pleasing *mezzo-forte*.

There is no need for rhythmic confusion over the final three bars, which are merely a general representation of the gentle ritenuto and diminuendo required at the end of the piece. Time needs to be taken, while ensuring that the melodic B in bar 25 is never obscured by the caressing broken chord that gradually surrounds it.

GRADE 5

Forward planning will be especially helpful when preparing for Grade 5. Around this time students often find that other commitments compete with their piano practice time. The inclusion of some light pieces that are quick to learn will help to maintain enjoyment in playing while the exam work is being systematically covered.

A:1 J. C. F. Bach *Allegretto in F*

This attractive piece by one of J. S. Bach's talented sons seems to epitomize the elegance and good manners that we associate with the eighteenth century. It is best suited to a sensitive player who will appreciate its lyrical beauty and unhurried grace.

The almost constant semiquaver movement and ornaments are determining factors in tempo choice, which should nevertheless flow easily with two, not four, main beats in a bar. However, students should not be put off by the seemingly complicated ornament realizations – if problematic they can be modified (or omitted, if necessary) in preference to disrupting the pulse in a struggle to fit in all the notes. The predominantly homophonic texture relies on good balance between the right-hand melody and its largely Alberti-style accompaniment. A well-developed cantabile will enable rich, song-like tone in the right-hand line. Although main dynamic contrasts are indicated, there is plenty of opportunity for rise and fall within phrases, especially at the appoggiaturas, with their sense of release after a clash of harmony. Keeping the fingers close to the keys will help to control the left-hand semiquavers, the first of which can be gently highlighted to convey the harmonic changes.

Good co-ordination will ensure that the 3rds at the opening sound exactly together, and an accurate downward leap in bar 16 is dependent on safe placing of the B♭ thumb note. Students with a limited hand-span may prefer to slide the thumb from B♭ to A for the 6ths later in the bar.

The generally higher register after the double bar seems to herald a lighter, more carefree mood. Couplet slurs, as suggested, give definition to the phrasing and, again, appoggiaturas at the end of each four bars will add further elegance if well-shaped. Students will be relieved to discover that the final eight bars are identical to bars 9–16 – but here a well-judged pacing of the last two bars will ensure a sensitively measured ending.

A:2 Beethoven *Minuet in D*

The two contrasted sections of this piece contain many of the hallmarks of the mature Beethoven while also showing the confidence and assertiveness of youth. This is exciting music which will appeal to students with dramatic flair, strong fingers and a good command of the keyboard.

The opening is characterized by strong rhythmic gestures which encompass a large range of the keyboard. Accenting the staccato quavers, keeping the semiquavers lighter, preserves the natural stress of the slurs. The sense of propulsion towards the *sforzando* (an editorial addition) at bar 3 is then balanced by a descent, which needs graceful tapering. The slurs here and elsewhere in the piece can be enhanced by 'block' pedalling, depressing on the first chord and releasing on the second. Left-hand dotted rhythms should have a percussionist's precision in bars 5–6, and departure from the tie must be exactly in time. Examining the harmonic progressions after the double bar reveals how Beethoven creates a sense of momentum which builds towards the unexpected 1st inversion E♭ major chord at bar 13. Well-defined right-hand semiquavers and ever stronger *sforzandi* will ensure that the climax has maximum impact. If the stretch is unmanageable, the four-note chords in bars 13–14 may be modified to omit the thumb notes in each hand.

The Trio section reveals a more tender aspect of the composer. There is no change of tempo here, but smoother chords, well-balanced to highlight the top note, together with a predominantly quiet dynamic, will achieve an effective contrast. The semi-staccato indication in bars 21–3 (and by implication in bars 29–31) suggests lightly detached chords, not too short but well-shaped. The different registers used in bars 25–8 hint at a quasi-orchestral texture, as if strings and woodwind are in dialogue. *Sforzando* markings should be considered within the *piano* context, and changes of hand-position need to be anticipated in order to avoid any hesitation. The da capo, which must be played, follows on without a break.

A:3 Handel *Allemande in A minor*

The intimate character of this lovely piece evokes a scene of informal music-making, perhaps for the entertainment of a group of friends. It may seem a straightforward option at first glance, but its gentle beauty and subtlety need a sensitive, musical student to bring it to life.

The tempo should be sufficiently leisurely to convey the undulating twists and turns of the right-hand line comfortably. The piece poses few rhythmic challenges; however, the opening semiquaver must be given its correct length, and carefully counted rests will ensure that the second half of the piece does not begin early.

An awareness of the subtle expressive range of the harpsichord, for which the piece was written, is the key to understanding the style. A smooth, yet cleanly articulated, right hand seems to suit the flowing, mellifluous shape. Any tonal inflections should be gently made, with no hint of unevenness in the sound as the hand changes position. Rising and falling sequences offer scope for terraced dynamics, e.g. in bars 3–4, and an echo in the second half of bar 14 would be effective. Ties also form an expressive feature throughout the piece. Listening to the long note rapidly decreasing in tone is the best guide to matching the semiquaver which follows. The faster detail in bars 14–15 and the ornaments throughout require confident finger agility and must be carefully paced. However, modifying the cadential ornaments at bars 7 and 17 in favour of the simpler realization in bar 6 may be a better option for some students. Lightly spreading the three-note chords would add further stylistic interest and prominence to the harmony.

The left hand plays an equally important role by highlighting the harmonic progressions and providing rhythmic interest. Imagining it played on the cello will give a clue to the phrasing. Detached quavers and short slurs, with a gentle stress on the first and third beats, is a stylish option which will provide an airy quality to the texture.

A:4 Bolck *Allegro vivo*

This piece has a fresh-faced charm and quick-wittedness which will appeal to students with the facility and athleticism to move quickly over the whole keyboard. Apart from a few passages midway, the melodic interest remains in the right hand and textures are straightforward and easy to manage.

Maintaining good rhythmic poise at a well-chosen tempo is central to success. Lightened second and third beats will give that all-important one-in-a-bar rhythmic lilt, and care will be needed to keep ends of phrases poised. Smooth, clear right-hand scales, carefully synchronized with the other hand, followed by crisply defined staccato chords will get the piece off to a stylish start. A light hand touch should be used for the chords, listening for all notes sounding, and the slur in bar 7 needs to be shaped elegantly. As the pitch starts climbing at bar 17, clean right-hand phrasing, which can be mirrored in the left hand, gives further elegance. Your student should make the most of the dynamic shifts every two bars and keep the left hand subservient to the right-hand soloist throughout the section.

After the double bar, further acrobatics occur as importance is shared more equally between the hands. Changes of clef need care and there must be no hesitation as the left hand leaps downwards. The section begins with a game of copycat after which the left hand assumes the role of soloist. Imagining this section transcribed for woodwind instruments might help bring the phrasing fully to life, flute articulating much of the upper detail, for example, while clarinet and bassoon share the sustained left-hand phrases.

Dynamics can be used to highlight the key changes in this section. Enjoy the F naturals in bar 57 and bars 61–2, and note that the F sharp printed in bar 58 is probably a mistake. The return to G major follows a similar pattern to the opening section, albeit in condensed form. The final semiquaver run can be approached either by making a slight ritardando or by staying in tempo, but the last chord should be kept short for full surprise effect.

A:5 J. G. Krebs *Allegro in G*

The attractive, outgoing character of this piece will suit students with good right-hand dexterity and the confidence to maintain momentum with little, if any, respite.

Tempo choice should reflect the allegro character without sounding hurried. A good sense of keyboard geography is needed to manage the changes of position, especially after the double bar. Quick, accurate movements, anticipating the new position, will ensure that no awkward hesitations occur between phrases.

As always in fast-running music, systematic right-hand fingering, well-rehearsed, is the key to a stumble-free performance, especially in the more chromatic figures which do not always lie easily under the fingers.

A harpsichord-like clarity can be produced by bright, crisp 'attack' from all fingers. Care is needed to avoid unwanted overlapping sounds, especially from the weaker fourth and fifth fingers. Various valid phrasing options might be considered for the semiquaver figuration. The printed couplet slurring, with its implication of detached non-phrased notes, will produce a high level of authentic detail; however, this may be beyond the skills of many students, in which case a generally smoother, yet clear, right-hand touch, using the slurs to 'point' the clashing appoggiaturas in the sequential phrases, might be the more straightforward option. A mixture of detached and slurred quavers will bring variety and rhythmic character to the left-hand accompaniment. Slurring the quavers in couplets highlights the rising sequences, and joining the 3rds in bars 17–20 is an effective choice.

Since the composer has provided almost no dynamic clues, there is considerable scope for exploring one's own ideas. Tracing the contours of the intricate, undulating right-hand line will help in finding its natural tonal rise and fall. Any use of *forte* should be within the tonal limitations of the instruments of the time, and tapered phrase-endings will lend gracefulness to the style. Treating the repetitions of phrases as echoes is a stylish option and the rising sequence at bars 5–7 etc. seems to imply a crescendo.

A:6 Rameau *La Joyeuse*

The busy athleticism of this joyful piece is best suited to a nimble-fingered student with plenty of agility. The almost constant quaver movement, and shifting between contrapuntal and homophonic textures, never allows the music to stand still for long.

Some detective work will reveal the structure of this rondo with its alternation between the opening eight-bar refrain and its two contrasting reprises. Care is needed to manage repeats seamlessly, in order to link the sections without hiatus. The small-printed Ds at the start which serve to complete the left-hand scales at the end of each reprise should be played.

Practising a D major scale in 3rds and 10ths is useful initial training for much of the figuration. Crisp articulation, lifting all fingers efficiently, is particularly important when the hands play close together. However, throughout the piece a harpsichord-like brilliance should be borne in mind.

A firm, authoritative touch will immediately capture the bright mood of the opening refrain. The falling quaver figures have their own natural shape as the hands play a chasing game, a feature which can be highlighted by detaching ends of phrases.

Starting the first reprise more quietly allows a terracing effect as the music shifts upwards to A major at bar 12. Here the texture is simpler, with the right-hand line taking precedence over its accompaniment. A mixture of detached and slurred crotchets gives interest to the gavotte-like rhythms, with all ornaments placed on, not before, the beat.

The shift to B minor provides a welcome change at the start of the second reprise. Here again, carefully controlled left-hand quavers at the start will give transparency to the texture before the contrapuntal texture resurfaces in bar 24. Finally, careful practice will ensure that the four-bar link to the final refrain, with its twists and turns, is safely negotiated.

Varying the approach to each appearance of the refrain – perhaps a slightly quieter second statement and a more emphatic final one – will add further freshness and interest to the performance.

B:1 MacDowell *To a Wild Rose*

One can imagine the composer on a woodland stroll discovering a single blossom and becoming lost in wonder at this specimen of nature's understated beauty. It is perhaps the viewer's sense of quiet delight that should be conveyed in performances of MacDowell's most popular composition.

Understanding the phrases will help your student to achieve a musical flow. Most of these are four bars long, despite the slur marks, so it is worth deciding where the phrase is leading. For example, the first phrase peaks gently at the beginning of bar 4, whereas the second peaks less perceptibly at bar 6 after which it fades into the perfect cadence of bars 7–8. The dynamic is mostly *piano* or quieter so fingers can be kept close to the keys for much of the time. Even the passage marked *forte* should not be overdone, although some arm weight will be needed. The intensity of bars 22–6 can be aided by a slight accelerando which will also highlight the subsequent ritardando.

Technically there are no big challenges, although a rearrangement of bar 41 will help smaller hands. In order to hold down the bass note A, it is a good plan to play the C♯ and middle A with the right hand, slightly separating the notes if need be. Melodic lines call for some projection and it is helpful to imagine that the relevant finger is heavier than its neighbours. Where two notes are to be sounded simultaneously, projection of the upper one can be practised outside the context of the piece. The focus is therefore on cultivating greater firmness in one fingertip than the other, thereby allowing the melody note a little extra impact.

Pedalling is straightforward throughout, the changes following the bar-by-bar harmonic progressions; changing with each crotchet in bars 41–3, however, may be desirable.

For those of a sensitive disposition, this delightful miniature is an ideal choice.

B:2 Schumann ***

Schumann often took an interest in composing music for children, and this charming 'song without words' helps the young player to develop a warm cantabile and a good sense of textural balance.

Clara Schumann's metronome suggestion works well as a basic tempo but some pliancy seems advisable. Phrase-endings in, for example, bars 3–4 can be helped by a judicious easing of the tempo, and a concluding ritenuto in bars 21–2 is appropriate. It could be beneficial to discuss the (mainly) four-bar phrase structure with your students, and help them to identify some highs and lows as well as the points of tension (for example, beats 1 and 2 of bar 2) and resolution (beats 3 and 4). Phrase contours may be reflected through dynamic nuances, although cantabile lines can be quite generous tonally, engaging a deep, firm touch.

A good textural balance is important and the quaver accompaniments should be kept discreet. Whichever finger is playing the tune will need a little more weight (and height above the key) than the others, particularly when the melody is in the left hand, as in bars 5–8. The opening indication *fp* is clearly impossible to achieve on a single note, so it is appropriate to interpret this as a direction to start *forte* and then make a diminuendo to *piano* by the end of bar 1. However, your student can lean into rather than hit the opening note, treating it as a gentle call to attention as opposed to a surprise assault.

When the music is harmonized, pedalling is desirable. Changing the pedal with each beat works in places such as bars 9–10, where foot action must be gentle (but precise) if a percussive effect is to be avoided. However, in other places, such as bars 2 and 6 the pedal can be held across two beats.

Given the enigmatic three stars of the original title, your students can have fun imagining what this music may represent.

B:3 Tárrega *Adelita*

This beautiful guitar miniature transfers very well to the piano and it will be enjoyed by all who relish subtle dance rhythms and attractive melodies. Its ABA (minor–major–minor) structure provides contrasting emotional landscapes which can be reflected in your student's interpretation. The repeat of the A section also facilitates the learning task.

The main technical challenge is the passage in 3rds in the middle section. Here, forearm, wrist and fingers need to operate in equilibrium, the fingers guiding the lateral movement into the correct keys while a relaxed forearm and wrist allow a gentle dropping sensation.

A tempo of crotchet = *c.*92 is suitable but the mazurka character will not be lost if the music is played just a little faster, perhaps at crotchet = *c.*104. A feeling of one rather than three beats per bar, with a gentle lean into the left-hand bass note, will enhance the musical lilt. There is also scope for rubato. For example, its subtle use in bars 4 and 20 can add expressive shape to the end of the phrase and help to ease in the repeat of the opening tune. Many guitarists apply plentiful rubato to bar 14 (marked *molto tenuto*) where lingering on the second beat in particular seems musically apt.

A singing tone is required in the right-hand part (which, according to the score, never drops much below *mezzo-piano*) and, while a seamless legato is desirable, clarity and focus in the tone are also important, bearing in mind the guitar original. Clear observation of the hairpins will enhance the phrasing and, as a practice measure, these nuances can be exaggerated to ensure their audibility before being moderated to suit the musical context. As suggested in the score, it is advisable always to play with the right hand at a dynamic level above that of the left so long as the latter provides enough harmonic support to keep the texture warm.

B:4 Gedike *Miniature*

Although entitled 'Miniature', this piece is quite rowdy and will benefit from an extrovert performance which projects its boisterous good humour. However, it also endorses the value of careful scale practice!

The music needs a one-in-a-bar feel, with many bars – for example bars 8–15 – requiring first-beat emphasis. A tempo of dotted crotchet = 84–88 seems suitable and there is no need to modify this anywhere except perhaps to allow for a slight placement of the first chord in bar 17 or to permit a minimal ritenuto in bar 36 to ease in the reprise. Occasional practice with a metronome may be beneficial to guard against rushing.

Few dynamics are marked and most indicate *forte* or above. However, to avoid too much 'shouting', it may be a good idea to moderate the *forte* tone in places. For example, a drop to *mezzo-piano* in bar 8 will enable an effective crescendo to bar 16 and, similarly, the dynamic level could be reduced at bar 25 to allow room for a general crescendo to *fortissimo*. During bars 59 to the end, where a crescendo from *piano* is marked, your student should not divulge too much too soon, always having something in reserve for the final, crowning *sff*.

Care is also needed over the contrasting articulations, especially in bars 8–15 and 44–52 where, every other bar, simultaneous legato and staccato articulations are called for in the right hand. As a primer, your student could practise this technique outside the context of the piece, perhaps striking two notes together, immediately and sharply releasing the lower of the two while holding on to the upper. A second note in the lower part could then be struck after the first for similar staccato release, and then a third, while ensuring that the upper note remains depressed.

A successful performance of this piece will require confidence – swagger even. The examiner should not be lulled to sleep!

B:5 Palmgren *Vestfinsk Dans (West-Finnish Dance)*

In stark contrast to the Gedike Miniature (B:4), the key words here are *con grazia*. Clearly this dance is one of restraint rather than bluster, charming the listener with its pastel shades. On a more pragmatic note, it is worth pointing out that no new musical material is introduced after bar 16.

Texturally, pedalling is an important element in this piece. Use of the pedal is desirable throughout, sometimes changing with each beat (as in bars 1–3), sometimes with each bar (as in 9–12), but always allowing harmonic coherence to be the final arbiter. In bar 13, where the pedal should ideally be changed on each beat, the right hand can take the second-beat D, thereby allowing the left hand to hold on to the bass G. The simplest solution to the textural challenge in bars 4 and 28 is to pedal through beats 1 and 2, changing on beat 3. By this means, the left hand is free to move away from the bass notes (G and D) without any loss of resonance.

Generally the top part carries the melody and there should be some projection of this, with the arm weight gently channelled down the outer fingers of the right hand. However, to preserve the soft colours it would be as well not to chisel out the melodic line too much, perhaps thinking of a flute rather than an oboe sound. Since no dynamic above *piano* is marked, arms can be kept light and still, and finger movements small, especially in the *pp dolce* section where use of the *una corda* pedal will also help. Some hairpin crescendos and diminuendos are indicated and these should be audible, so exaggerating the dynamic rise and fall while practising might be beneficial; in performance, however, the sound does not need to rise above *mezzo-piano*.

Your students may be able to sooth their listeners with this music. Prompting them to dance is a less likely outcome!

B:6 Tchaikovsky *Douce rêverie (Daydream)*

To reflect the freewheeling nature of daydreams, performances of this piece will benefit from a sense of improvisation, not to mention a refined command of phrasing and tonal balance.

Tempo rubato will often be appropriate and can be applied in places such as the two-bar phrase units in bars 1–8 and later similar stretches. Here, a very slight increase and decrease in tempo – and dynamic – seems appropriate to highlight the rising and falling contour of the right-hand melody. To avoid predictability, not every phrase need be thus shaped and, for example, bars 7–8 can generally go a little slower to ease in the reprise. (And the good news is that a lot of the material is repeated.)

Melodic playing needs an expressive cantabile which remains mellow, the tone being coaxed from the piano rather than forced, whatever the dynamic. Where a note is repeated across the bar, the first note should be held as long as is feasible before quickly lifting the finger to re-sound it. Adroit pedalling will conceal any residual gap in the line. Your students will also need to be aware that the left hand sometimes plays a countermelody (for example in bars 1–5). This needs to be audible (though not dominant), so the accompanying quaver chords should be struck from as close to the key as possible to ensure minimal sound. The latter will also be the case for right-hand playing in general when the left hand has the main melody, as in bars 17–21.

Dynamics are clearly marked in the score but it is worth remembering the daydream context when judging the *forte* tone. Even in places such as bars 21–2 where *forte* is shown accompanied by accents, a bell-like sonority seems called for. The music cannot be played effectively without using the sustaining pedal more-or-less throughout, and if harmonic changes are allowed to dictate pedal changes all should be well.

C:1 Darius Brubeck *For Lydia*

This is a tricky little number, but it's great fun to play once the rhythm has been thoroughly absorbed. The aim will be to *feel* the beat and syncopation rather than just count. However, unless your student is a natural jazz player, counting (and possibly help from a metronome) will be necessary at first. Players must be particularly alert to the rhythm when moving from bars 3 to 4, and again in bar 11.

As the left hand acts as the rhythm section, it would be wise to begin there. Care is needed over the articulation of the repetitive opening figure. Your student should drop into the first note of the slur, the tie and the fourth-beat accent, allowing the hand to rise a little with the thumb notes. The last two notes of the bar (A and G) can both be played by the thumb, thus helping to keep the hand relaxed and minimizing the stretch into the next bar. For similar reasons it would be helpful to give the fourth-beat quaver G of bar 3 to the right hand. Adding right hand later will be relatively easy except where there is a conflict of articulation – staccato against legato.

When working on the first section, the pedal should be added to the left hand when it feels secure enough. In addition to the given pedalling, there are other places that would benefit from its use. Assuming that most upbeat quavers will be staccato (like the first phrase), the pedal can be depressed on the first beat of bar 9 (and bar 10) and released with the staccato chord. Pedal can be even more useful in bar 11. Changing on the second half of beats 2, 3 and 4 will enable the harmony to be clear and allow the left hand more time to reach the lower notes. Pedal changes on the offbeat chords in the penultimate bar will contribute to a strong climax.

C:2 Kabalevsky *Kavaleriiskaya (Cavalryman)*

Few could fail to enjoy this exciting ride. Dramatic dynamic contrasts, a distinctly Russian melody and a motoric rhythmic drive vividly portray the horseman in this splendid piece. This is one for the confident, extrovert student.

A strong left hand will be needed, and care should be taken over all the articulation marks – accents, staccato and slurs – that give this piece so much of its character. Notes with accents, as in bars 7 and 8, can be slightly detached. An awareness of the sudden changes in dynamics should be a priority right from the start, too. Once the melody of the first section has been learnt, slow practice will help to develop controlled co-ordination when the offbeat chords are added.

The right hand takes over with a new theme at bar 26, but still has to manage some notes of the accompaniment. This whole middle section, especially bars 38 and 39 where the melody rises to A♭, can be made easier by redistributing some of the notes. This will be especially helpful for players with smaller hands. Put as simply as possible, the left hand may take all F and G♭ notes from the right-hand part between bars 26 and 40. This will enable the right hand to produce good tone for the melody and use more comfortable fingering. For instance, the second finger can be located over C for the first ten bars leaving the thumb to play the occasional A♭ and B♭ very lightly. From bar 36 to bar 39 the fourth finger will be over F, with a final shift to place third finger on C in bar 40.

A fast tempo will eventually be required, but it must always be rhythmic and controlled. A tempo of about crotchet = 126 is enough to convey the excitement of the music.

C:3 Villa-Lobos *Samba-lelê*

'Samba-lelê' is one of the popular children's songs that Villa-Lobos collected. It is a singing game where the children dance in a circle, acting out the various events of the story with the aid of a handkerchief. Your student might like to imagine some ideas to fit the music.

The tempo mark of *Poco lento* is a little deceptive, but the two-in-a-bar beat (minim = *c.*60) gives the vitality needed for a samba. In the ten-bar introduction, the left-hand drone bass should be kept quieter than the right, and the accents confined to the top note of the chords. The ostinato quaver figures heard throughout the piece help to propel the music forward but should be kept light and rhythmic.

The song begins at bar 11, and it would be helpful to practise it alone at first, following it as it moves up and down between the staves. The minim E (bar 12) is the strongest note of the phrase, and many will find it easier to take it with the right hand. The leap to the quavers above would soon become secure. Similarly, the D in bar 14 could receive the same treatment even though the chord there is more manageable.

For the first 18 bars the pedal only needs to be changed on first beats, but at bar 19 there is a different character to the music and pedalling becomes more spasmodic. This is the 'chorus' of the song, and the words 'Samba, samba, Samba-lelê' can be heard in the rhythm. As marked, the right-hand chords should be slightly accented and detached. In bars 20–22 (and similar) the pedal can be depressed just after the third beat and released on the first beat of the next bar. This will add a lift to the dance.

For exam purposes the repeat (*D.S. al Fine*) should not be played. Everything has already been repeated, and presumably further repetition was only needed to accommodate all the verses of the song.

C:4 A. Benjamin *Haunted House*

If you are looking for something out of the ordinary for a student who enjoys a joke, look no further. Arthur Benjamin is best known for his popular *Jamaican Rumba*, and as a result of the publicity it brought to Jamaica, the Jamaican government sent the composer a barrel of rum every year!

This particular piece could be background music for a cartoon film, and a lot of fun could be had inventing a story for it. Dynamics will be very important. The basic dynamic level is either *piano* or *pianissimo*, and there should be only a slight crescendo employed in bar 2 (and similar). Against this sinister background the sudden stabs of sound marked *sff* (bars 4 and 8) or *crescendo molto* (bars 11 and 12) will be really startling. The use of augmented 4ths and 5ths, together with slithering chromatic figures, adds to the ominous atmosphere.

The principal theme (bars 1–4) appears five times; first on G, then a tone lower on F. After a scary second idea (bars 9–14) that is full of alarming crashes and screams, the first theme returns, coloured by the *una corda* pedal. This time it starts on B but has subtle changes to the first few intervals – look out for the last note in bar 22 which could be mistaken for a C♮. The theme's last appearance is exactly as the original but now an octave lower and accompanied by a menacing chromatic figure.

There will be a temptation to play the C pedal note in bar 30 loudly, but the surprise should be saved for the dissonant chords marked *forte* and *pianissimo*. This is the only place where the sustaining pedal is used, and a keen ear will be needed to judge just how loudly and quietly these chords can be played – it should sound as though the second one is an eerie echo. With the *una corda* pedal still depressed, the last few bars just slip away into silence.

C:5 Milhaud *Modéré*

Ever since Mendelssohn's first set of *Songs without Words* was published in 1832, the form and title have been used by many other composers. Mendelssohn wrote that 'What the music I love expresses to me, is not thought too *indefinite* to put into words, but on the contrary, too *definite*.'

The first of French composer Darius Milhaud's set of four wordless songs sounds like a loving conversation between two people. It flows along in four-bar phrases in the form of a canon, and a metronome mark of crotchet = 60–66 would create an unhurried tempo. The main challenge is to control the tone of the left hand's answering phrases (at bar 3 and similar) because of the wider stretches involved. Ultimately this depends on perfect legato pedalling, but first it would be helpful to practise just the melody lines. The right hand begins and is then joined by the left at bar 3. Your student should listen to the way the voices weave in and out in imitation.

Dynamics should not be extreme, and a gentle rise and fall that follows the melodic shapes will give expression to the overlapping phrases. Each tied note should be given a little extra weight so that it is still heard as the harmony changes. At bar 13 the voices sing together until the first tune reappears in bar 17. Once the ear has learnt how the melodies *should* sound, there is a better chance of managing the balance when the accompaniment is added.

The next stage would be to practise each hand alone (with pedal added), giving special attention to the left hand. Simple legato pedalling, changing on every crotchet beat, is all that is required, but in bar 3 (and similar) the minim D♭ must be held through the pedal change on the second beat. Only then can the thumb move up to the tied note. A *poco ritenuto* through the last three bars will bring the piece peacefully to rest.

C:6 Christopher Norton *Sierra*

Christopher Norton's music is always popular, especially with teenagers who yearn for something that is cool. This is the piece for them.

The metronome mark of crotchet = *c.*126 (not dotted crotchet as printed) may seem fast at first for a piece marked 'calmly', and it could be some time before the quavers flow easily at that speed. It would be useful to learn the left hand and pedalling first, using slowly swinging arm movements from chord to chord while lightly tapping a crotchet beat with the spare foot or hand. Later it will be better to feel the piece as two- or even one-in-a-bar. Pedalling is clearly marked and should present little difficulty.

The rhythm of the right hand needs care, and further tapping (or use of a metronome set at a modest tempo) will help here. The principal melody (bars 1–8) has a pentatonic flavour, and it would be wise to incorporate dynamic marks and accents right from the start. With such a lavish use of pedal, there is a danger that the texture may become muddy, and only a skilful use of dynamic shading will produce the transparency the piece clearly needs.

At bar 9 the principal theme begins again but soon develops into another theme which gradually builds in excitement until reaching a climax in bars 19 and 20. Here it will be easier to time the triplet crotchets if counting is now two-in-a-bar. The tension subsides in bar 22 where a *poco ritenuto* would help to announce the reprise of the first melody at bar 23. Fingering is generally uncomplicated, but for the last two bars a neat sequence of 5-2-3-1 will ensure a smooth flow for the descending quavers. The arch-like form of the whole piece is underlined by its dynamics, so your student should hold the pause at the end and let the notes drift hazily away.

GRADE 6

Your student will now have achieved success in Grade 5 Theory, Practical Musicianship or Jazz. The assessment criteria at Grades 6–8 are more demanding than at the lower grades, so do make sure that you are familiar with them. At Grade 6, examiners will be looking for musical character, expression and style to be presented with greater conviction. Technical fluency will be needed to support the successful realization of these ideas.

A:1 J. S. Bach *Invention No. 14 in B flat*

'The Inventions' provide a wonderful introduction to Bach's contrapuntal style and this one is sure to be popular with candidates. It will require agile fingers, though, with well-matched hands and reliable co-ordination.

Articulation is a matter of taste, and one of the first things to do is to discuss with your student how the various figures may be played. Making the quavers detached is one method that is frequently employed. Another effective way is to play the semiquavers staccato while *most* of the quavers are legato. In this case the quavers best detached include the first in bars 1 and 6 and the first in bars 9, 10 and 11. Quavers that leap an octave and those that precede tied notes would also be detached. Legato can then be used to highlight the important four-note motif first heard in the left hand (bars 1–3) and then in the right. Similar phrasing can be employed with the quavers in bars 9–11, splitting the groups of four so that they all begin on an offbeat. Whatever is decided, it is essential that the articulation is consistent in both hands throughout the piece.

Once the piece begins to take shape, decisions will need to be taken over dynamics, too. There are many possibilities, but let the music suggest what might work. In this period it was customary to begin a lively piece *forte*, and as the elaborate principal figure (bar 1, right hand) is arc-like in shape, this suggests a rise and fall in the tone to match. Then as it proceeds sequentially with each repetition starting lower, a diminuendo may be effective. This would lead to a quieter level at bar 4 where the texture is thinner. When the music passes through minor keys a darker tone quality would be appropriate, and so on. This process is rather like a detective searching for clues!

The most challenging passages are in the second half (from bar 12) where thematic fragments chase each other in close canon, so slow practice is advisable. Even when the main theme returns complete and in the home key (middle of bar 16), the canon continues until a triumphant conclusion is reached.

A:2 J. L. Dussek *Rondo*

It would be a pity if the sheer length of this movement prevented your student from choosing to play it, for it is full of charm and good humour. In fact, as a typical rondo, there are not as many notes to learn as the first glance might suggest. The main theme is played five times with very few alterations, and the second theme appears twice (bars 9 and 60), unusually in the same key(s) both times.

The composer has indicated some subtle differences in texture which should be observed. From bar 13 to bar 18 the bass notes are sustained (in effect what is sometimes called 'finger-pedalling') and the same happens again when the passage returns at bar 64. However, a similar accompaniment that appears in the central episode at bar 37 should be played as written – without sustaining the bass notes. This creates a lighter, more buoyant sound. In bars 5–7 the lines of dotted crotchets (alto and bass voices) should be played as legato as possible. The bass line can be entirely joined if the fourth finger is turned over the fifth from C to the B♭, with the repeated quavers above played staccato. This would then cover any slight gaps in the alto line. There is really very little scope for pedal in this movement if clarity is to be maintained, so it is worth cultivating a good legato where needed.

The metronome mark of dotted crotchet = *c.*76 may feel a little fast for some and a tempo of about dotted crotchet = 66 may be preferable. The performance needs to be lively but gracious and expressive, too. There are plenty of dynamic marks to provide colour, and the gentle rise and fall of the phrasing should be appropriately shaped. In contrast there are moments of exuberance when semiquaver runs must sparkle. The third theme forms the middle episode and begins with the upbeat into bar 29; this melody (in A♭ major) needs to dance gracefully. Although the themes are closely related, they all have different characters – much like the members of any family.

This is a piece that will give much pleasure and is well worth the effort of learning.

A:3 J. C. Kellner *Fugue*

A fugue at Grade 6 may seem quite a challenge, but this is not J. S. Bach. This one, in three voices, has a comparatively undemanding texture and provides an excellent introduction to the form.

A basic outline of the fugue is given in the footnote, and, as with any contrapuntal piece, the first thing to do is to play each voice through on its own to see what adventures it has. It is a good idea to mark where all the entries of the subject (and answer) occur. There are only seven appearances that are complete (bars 1, 3, 7, 10, 17, 25 and 29) and these should all be prominent, though not necessarily loud. For instance, the one in A minor (starting at the end of bar 17) would be effective at *mezzo-piano* level, while the alto voice above is played *piano*. The strongest tone might be reserved for the last appearance of the subject in the bass (bar 29). The partial stretto passages, where entries pile up on one another, create their own dynamic shaping (e.g. the last three quavers of bar 19 through to bar 25). Elsewhere, sequential counterpoint in the episodes may be coloured by diminuendo or crescendo.

As with dynamics, decisions must be made about the articulation. The subject sounds well if it is all legato, but some might choose to play a few (or all) of the quavers staccato. The character of the theme changes accordingly. Before practice begins in earnest, it would be fun to experiment with different versions; however, once the matter is settled, articulation must be consistent throughout, so it should not be made too complicated! There are some upbeat quavers that are best detached. These often mark the beginnings of new phrases (e.g. the F♯ in bar 3 and D in bar 5) or cadences (e.g. the octave D jump in bar 10 and similar one in bar 21).

The climax of the fugue is reached in bar 38. The tempo should pull back a little as the spread chord is approached, and the pause held dramatically. The original tempo should only be resumed after the quaver rest has made its impact.

A:4 T. Arne *Presto*

The exuberance and sparkle of this sonata movement make it an appealing choice, especially for the student who has agile fingers. Almost entirely in two-part counterpoint, it is harmonically uncomplicated and lies comfortably under the hands.

Semiquavers need a crisp attack, the fingers striking from just a little above the keys, while supporting quavers, as in bars 4 and 13, should be lightly detached. There are only a few ornaments, and where the trill appears over a semiquaver (e.g. bars 2 and 3) it is perfectly acceptable to play a simple acciaccatura. Those placed over quavers require a four-note 'short trill' starting on the upper note. If the left-hand trills (bars 11 and 12) prove a hindrance, it would be better to omit them – indeed, they do not appear in some editions. In bar 18, instead of a trill, try a four-note turn; it makes a comfortable link to the following note.

Unless an editor has been at work supplying dynamics, the movement will appear without any. When played on the piano it would sound dull without them, however, so ask your student to contribute some ideas on the subject. In this period it was usual to begin a piece *forte*, especially in such a brilliant movement. Sequential figures can be shaped with crescendos and diminuendos, either employing terraced dynamics or by a steady increase or decrease in tone. At bars 19 and 20 there should be a feeling of stress on the first beat and release of tension on the third as the harmony resolves. It would also be effective to make a crescendo in bar 21 so that the return of the first theme and home key is positive.

If the score has no given fingering, it must be worked out before serious practice begins so that the semiquaver figures flow evenly and securely. When patterns are repeated finger sequences should be used wherever possible, and at bar 13, as the hands briefly overlap, the left hand is best placed above the right.

A metronome mark of crotchet = *c*.96 will have the music dancing along brightly and buoyantly, and a *poco ritenuto* over the last three chords will make for a decisive finish.

A:5 Haydn *Andante in D*

It would be helpful to listen to a recording of the second movement of Haydn's Symphony No. 81 before embarking on this charming keyboard transcription. It is a siciliano with variations and will need a graceful, lilting tempo. A metronome mark of quaver = *c*.96 works well, but ultimately it should be felt as a swaying two-in-a-bar.

The theme itself is not difficult; only the turn in bar 4 might prove to be troublesome, and would be better omitted if it becomes a stumbling-block. The mood is amiable, and the ornaments and more decorated passages should be kept light and buoyant. Pedal will help to create legato lines where appropriate throughout the movement, but it should be used sparingly and never allowed to cover rests or the natural breathing spaces at ends of phrases.

The first variation begins with the upbeat into bar 13, and as the music becomes more florid and technically demanding, it will be essential to establish reliable fingering right from the start. For instance, in the second half of bar 22, the descending broken-thirds figure is best played with the conventional 1-4-2-3 sequence which fits very neatly here. Another 'classical' fingering can be employed in bars 45 and 46 where a rising broken-chord passage needs the utmost agility. Prepare by placing second finger on the upbeat A♯ before using 1-2-4-1-2-4-2-4-5 twice, and in the next bar 1-2-3-2-3-5-1-2-3. This third variation (beginning with the upbeat to bar 37) is quite virtuosic and it would be easier to manage if some parts were memorized.

The dramatic heart of the movement is the second variation where the mode changes to minor. Your student should make the most of the contrasts between the strong outbursts and soothing answers, and between detached and legato phrases. Notice needs to be taken of the weeping chromatic figure at bar 29, the Neapolitan colouring in bar 31, and the chords in bars 33–4 that rise to an anguished diminished 7th – so many gestures to enjoy in just a few bars.

Once the brilliance of the third variation fades, the movement is rounded off by a return to the theme in its original simplicity.

A:6 D. Scarlatti *Sonata in C minor*

One of the most well-known and beautiful of Scarlatti's keyboard sonatas, this is sure to be a popular alternative choice.

Sometimes ornaments are omitted in the initial stages of learning, but in this case it would be wise to include them straight away. They are not difficult and are an essential part of the melody. Consisting of eight demisemiquavers (including the two written in the score), they all begin on the upper note. The only ornament that differs is in bar 20 where the trill is over a dotted crotchet. It would be effective to linger a little on the auxiliary note (E♭) and finish the trill on the third beat.

The first theme's gently undulating outline would benefit from nuances that rise and fall to match, and a legato touch would be suitable for both hands. The second theme starts with the upbeat into bar 5 and is quite spiky in character. This feature can be highlighted by using staccato on all the quavers except for the one on the third beat which might sound better slurred to the following semiquavers. There is an opportunity to use echo dynamics in bars 5–8, although a stepwise crescendo leading to the high point in bar 9 would also be effective. Whatever is decided, the range of dynamics should be kept fairly narrow for this period of keyboard music.

Fingering will need care in the legato passages, and in a few places it helps to reallocate notes from one hand to the other. For instance, in bars 3 and 4, third beat, the right hand could take the upper G of the left hand's octave, using fingers 4/2 on the B and G, and in bar 24 the left hand could play the last two notes of the fourth-beat trill, making it easier to negotiate the leap into the next bar. Another awkward corner may be smoothed by swapping the hands over. In bar 18 the main melody passes from left hand to right on the third beat, so a wide jump mid-phrase can be avoided if the right hand takes all the upper notes in that bar.

A metronome mark of crotchet = *c.*76 will allow the piece to dance gracefully.

B:1 Brahms *Waltz in A flat*

Many will be familiar with the melody of this piece, which is full of lullaby character, gently persuasive and song-like with warm harmonies. As a consequence, however, it needs the most subtle treatment, with a supple, relaxed physical approach in order to avoid angularity or harshness.

The two hands require entirely different sound-worlds so are best approached separately. The right hand is both melody and accompaniment, and the solo top line supported by the underlying harmonic notes should be clearly defined. The overall tone and legato is easier with a slightly flatter hand shape, using the resistance of the key surface to control the sound as well as a pliant 'give' in the wrist, particularly on the first beats of a bar and on larger chords. Lateral movement is needed, particularly in the final two lines, to avoid the triplet 6ths sounding disjointed and 'academic'.

The left hand presents different challenges, not least in its association with the pedal. There needs to be harmonic support from the bass notes, the pedal used throughout the bar initially (changing on the first beat and after the sound of the note), but later sometimes on each chord (as in bar 14). Personal taste will decide whether or not to pedal the chords individually in bars 3, 7 etc. but the piece will sound over-pedalled if the chords on the second and third beats are too bold or the harp-like, arpeggiated indications are ignored. These are there to prevent a hard-edged start to the chords, softening further the beginnings of notes. Holding the bass notes just a little longer, allowing the wrist to drop before moving to the chords, gives time for a slower, subtle pedal change.

The tempo will depend on the performer's ability to control the sound and pedal as well as on the piano and the acoustic, but the piece mustn't ever sound hurried or agitated. Taking time, and placing chords around 'corners' and at climaxes of phrases such as bar 13, will avoid the need to be too loud in dynamic, keeping all the musical decision-making in context.

A small ritenuto towards the end would allow a beautiful decrescendo through the final chords and, if lightly lifted, the final bar will imply that the piece continues forever, if only in the memory.

B:2 Granados *Danza de la rosa (Dance of the Rose)*

It is hard not to be seduced by this poetic and very beautiful dance, which, while being full of Spanish sunshine, has nevertheless a poignancy and underlying sadness.

The opening is fairly optimistic in personality. The melody needs a vocal sense of line with a light accompaniment supported by legato pedal throughout – changing after the chord sounds to hold it through the bar. The pedal lift between bars 3 and 4 may be omitted if the balance is well-controlled. The left hand's top Fs need to be kept subtle and soft; being above the predominant texture they risk sounding bell-like. Technical work and listening will be needed to control the balance in the right hand where the underlying chords must never interfere with the tune. The grace notes should have a lightness and ease, tucked in without disturbing the pulse.

A melancholy shadow creeps into bar 9, and taking a little time to place the B♭ minor chord will herald a rather tearful middle section. Here, the three-bar phrases valiantly grasp at something more tangible, but it doesn't quite convince, hence the *poco rall.* in bar 16. Some rubato is effective in this reflective section and careful listening through the ascending arpeggio of bar 13 will prevent it detracting from the melodic B♭. For clarity and effect the grace notes here might be lightly played *on* the beat and before the pedal is back down; in bar 13, therefore, the pedal lifts after the left hand's G♭, the grace notes are played while the left hand holds its note, and the pedal is depressed the moment that the melodic note is established.

From bar 17 it may help to play the melody on its own several times, making a mental template of how it will sound and its length of phrase; immediately introducing the accompaniment, which needs quite demanding control, may overly influence the musical decision-making. The first melodic note might be brought in after the spread dotted minims in bar 17 to convey the beginning of the melody and, again, awareness of balance is important, adjusting if the accompaniment becomes too intrusive.

The final bars are truly wonderful – the first G like a bell, followed by a vocal cry from the heart before drifting once more into a sad sleep.

B:3 Schumann *Fürchtenmachen (Frightening)*

How well Schumann, a dedicated father, understood a child's mind! This piece so clearly depicts the haunting terror of the bad dreams of childhood. The suspense of the chromatic and torturous lines in the opening section, the breathless chase of the second, and the typically incongruous character of the dream's middle part marvellously conjure up our common experiences.

While there are many technical challenges it is the mental agility needed to move quickly from one mood to another that makes the piece so difficult to play. Imagery, storytelling and preparing ahead are all so important in bringing the piece to life with conviction.

The opening should have a conscientious finger legato throughout, a seamless blending of the left-hand 3rds, listening to the release of the previous notes; this will avoid the need for too much depth of pedal movement. Dabs of pedal here and there to warm the tone and a true legato in the right hand will enable a clearly voiced and shaped melody without too much interference from the harmonies. There are no rules of pedal here, and the performer will need to adapt to the instrument and room.

With the change of scene at the second section the left hand is clearly the important line, dictating both the tempo and rhythmic drive. The right-hand chords should be very light, hand ready in advance, and co-ordination completely at ease; some 'shadow jumping' or playing the chords on the beat will help with familiarity. The final accented quaver B – 'off we go again' – is a breathless pause before the second repeat. All repeats are needed in the exam.

The middle section after the Tempo I reprise is brighter and provides some light relief. The *sforzando* chords should not be spiteful or heavy but short with maybe a dab of direct pedal, and the brief semiquaver figures can be dynamically shaped, perhaps decreasing in volume from the first chord. In bars 25–8 the more optimistic character slips away, with left-hand chords unobtrusive and pedal used each beat – before the nightmare returns.

The semiquaver rest in the penultimate bar serves as a quick check that it has all been a dream before the comforting final perfect cadence.

B:4 Beethoven *Andante*

The emotional impact of this beautiful miniature movement will only be truly appreciated upon hearing the full sonata. The juxtaposition of its G minor key against the G major of the outer movements gives the opening poignancy, and the middle section's contrast of E♭ major adds warmth and generosity to the spirit of the piece. It is a song without words, and, at the opening, perhaps a duet.

The 9/8 key signature belies a feel of three-in-a-bar, which is essential to the natural sense of line; it shouldn't seem 'counted' in quavers. The semiquavers must also be taken into account since they must not sound hurried or anxious. These considerations will allow the performer to arrive at a fairly decisive 'right' tempo.

If students can convincingly project the top notes of the right-hand chords and sustain a sense of line, the sound-world will be there for a musically persuasive performance. The balance needed can first be found by playing the chords as a duet with two hands; various strategies then need to be employed to achieve the same sound within the one hand.

A subtle, unobtrusive left hand will enhance the melody's shape and projection. The roots of the harmonies should be slightly bolder and supportive and the other notes (e.g. repeated Ds in bar 1) extremely light – a gentle heartbeat giving a natural flow but never obscuring the held melodic notes. Keeping the weight towards the outside of the hand and holding the root note with the finger through the rest of the beat will help. The latter in addition allows greater freedom with the pedal, the use of which is essential to achieve warmth and harmonic support.

Rubato will enhance the magic moments – with time particularly to be taken over the florid right hand in bar 19 where the rhythmic outline strongly suggests a holding-back before moving forward to the top F. Time is also needed to portray the unexpected move to a D major chord in bar 21.

When the flow of the accompaniment stops in the final two bars this should not sound sudden or awkward. The chords need space and time, as if making the final but most important statement of the narrative.

B:5 Chopin *Mazurka in A flat*

One of the lesser known of Chopin's mazurkas, this is nonetheless an alluring, enticing piece which offers a chance to explore the composer's rich, sometimes chromatic language within a Polish dance form that he made his own. It is full of repetition and seductive sequences, with effectively only 30 bars to learn. Unusually, it does not have the mazurka's characteristic dotted rhythm but the idiomatic second and third beat emphases are there in abundance.

Not a fast dance, it requires only a moderate tempo and gentle three-in-a-bar as well as some rubato to colour the changes and add interest. This is particularly true of the opening bars which could so easily sound like a Hanon exercise. A crescendo and sense of movement towards the first beat of bar 3, then a relaxation and diminuendo, will help, although it is crucial that a clear pulse is established in the introductory bars.

Chopin's phrasing is significant, needing interpretation within the context of the dance. The two-bar phrases of the opening melody should be lightened at the end of the phrase, contrasting with the 'stamp of the foot' in bar 10, where the phrase is foreshortened; a lift before the second-beat chord can suggest the accent. Bars 14 to 17 are an embellishment of the preceding bars, and so the contrasting articulation of the quavers is particularly important – but they mustn't sound mechanical. The middle section's phrasing naturally implies the third-beat accent.

Control and subtlety of pedal and balance will make or break the performance. Touches of pedal are needed throughout, not just where marked, and mostly across the first two beats. To enable independence of the foot, however, all legato lines and held chords must be achieved by the fingers; significant practice without pedal is therefore invaluable. This is particularly true of bars 14 to 17 where the underlying harmonies need to be held with the fingers under the staccato quavers; minims are also held in bars 21, 23 etc.

A clear, projected melodic line with persuasive dynamic shape, and light second and third beats, will add elegance and charm as the piece ends with what can only be described as a nineteenth-century 'fade out'.

B:6 S. Heller *Etude in D*

This is a beautiful piece from a poetic and still under-performed composer. While Heller's compositions are much used as teaching exercises, they are far more than this. Here, just like Chopin (his friend), Heller transcends the title 'Etude', composing something of much greater musical depth.

There are three essential elements to consider – the melody, accompaniment and bass line – and it is the control and independence of this texture that will communicate the performer's interpretation to the audience. With thoroughly organized fingering each finger can be trained to do its part, and learning the piece without pedal will ensure that all the held melodic notes in both hands are controlled and sustained by the fingers, the hands independent of each other.

At the same time the tonal control of the accompaniment needs to be refined, with the right hand's melodic lines projected above the accompanying semiquavers, and clearly and boldly shaped. Excellent practice for this is to take a phrase and educate the fingers to project each textural aspect in turn, all other parts *pianissimo*. This will encourage the fine motor control needed to embrace the world of colour and tonal nuance here.

Achieving this control will also enable the finer subtleties to be explored – just how much tone to give to left-hand melodic lines, and how much dynamic contrast and shape. The semiquaver accompaniment must not dictate the dynamic, however, so a *forte* with this texture should never be robust, and articulation always interpreted within the overall dynamic. The left hand in bars 18 and 19, for example, needs to be brighter and marginally detached but not heavily accented or loud.

Subtle pedalling is necessary, and practice done without pedal will reveal where it is most helpful or, conversely, where it risks spoiling the overall character. In general, legato pedalling with each crotchet or from quaver to quaver will enhance most of the piece but only small dabs are needed to colour bars 32, 34 and 36.

For a musical and talented student this emotional song without words is a perfect choice. It will inspire and encourage a subtlety of control and colour which approaches the realms of the professional world of piano playing.

C:1 L. Berkeley *Allegro*

This colourful and lively piece is a good introduction to the spiky, neo-classical world of English composer Lennox Berkeley. It will suit those students to whom clarity of articulation and texture comes more naturally than romantic warmth.

An obvious feature is the restlessly changing metre in which crotchet lengths occurring at or near the end of the bar will need special care. The bars in which all the quavers are sounded present less challenge, although it is worth clapping out the rhythms of, for example, bars 8–10. This will help to develop the feeling of gradually diminishing bar lengths and a shifting downbeat emphasis. The metre is thus allowed its particular character and an undifferentiated series of quaver pulses in performance is avoided.

Articulation is an important feature, especially for the slurred couplets which occur throughout. Your student can practise these by dropping into the first note from a height above the keyboard appropriate to the marked dynamic, then deftly lifting out of the second note, engaging little more than the weight of the finger. Where contrasting articulations between the hands are concerned, single-handed practice is of limited value because it is the physical sensation of opposition that must be assimilated. It may therefore be advantageous to divide, for example, bar 17 into three units – quavers 1–3, quavers 4–5 and quaver 6 – and concentrate exclusively on how the legatos, staccatos and accent combine. The 3rds in bars 13–14 may prove challenging and it should be helpful when practising to focus on down–up motions from a loose wrist rather than on lateral movements which might encourage tension and unevenness.

The dynamics are all clearly labelled but it is worth bearing in mind that the loudest is saved for last; so the earlier *forte* dynamic might be adjusted accordingly. The *forte* tone benefits from a slightly edgy quality so firmness of touch is desirable as long as the sound does not become ugly. This is a danger in music which is written predominantly in two parts and in which no pedalling is actually necessary.

A neat, effectively coloured performance of this piece will round off a Grade 6 programme very nicely.

C:2 Jason Rebello *A Wise Bud*

This easy-going jazz-inspired piece, with its catchy rhythms and melodies, should prove a popular choice. However, its relative brevity and uncluttered appearance contain some definite challenges.

As with all swung music, catching the authentic idiom can prove elusive. Listening to masters of jazz – such as this work's dedicatee, the bebop pianist Bud Powell, or to Rebello himself in, for example, *Monty's Blues* – can be instructive. The triplet feeling should not be too classical and it is often appropriate to give the shorter note a slight 'kick' so that the flow is not too smooth. Scatting the syllables (to 'doo-ba-doo-ba' or similar) can be a useful way of getting the feel of, for instance, bars 29–31. Accenting offbeats can also complement the style, and the chords in bars 8 and 16, the right-hand C in bar 6 and the left-hand F♯ in bar 20 seem typical places for this treatment. A very slightly detached manner of playing the right-hand part may also help to define the style.

Some of the music is heavily syncopated, so organizing the rhythms around a slow metronome tick may be a useful preliminary tactic, although eventually the beat should be 'felt' if the style is to come across convincingly. The pulse needs to be stable throughout and practising on a keyboard to a synthesized swing backing could be helpful – better still if your student knows a jazz drummer with whom to rehearse.

In keeping with the genial nature of the music, there is probably no need to play especially loudly at any point, and an overall dynamic level of *mezzo-piano* to *mezzo-forte* seems appropriate. Your student may wish to differentiate the middle eight (bars 17–24) by adopting a different general dynamic, either louder or quieter according to preference. While it is helpful to have a dynamic scheme in mind it is also fitting to leave some of the detail to the spur of the moment, as long as the musical style has been sufficiently studied and absorbed.

Finally, your student should make sure that the accidentals are carefully checked and retained through the bar – it would be a shame if Rebello's juicy jazz chords were compromised in the exam room!

C:3 Trad. Chinese, arr. Zhang Zhao *Jingpo shan ge (Jingpo Folksong)*

This piece presents a good opportunity to study pentatonic composition. The melody is based mostly on the A minor pentatonic scale, although this drops a semitone to G♯ in bars 31–45. A lot of the music is thus played on the white notes which should aid the learning process.

Generally the right-hand touch can be bright and incisive (whatever the dynamic level), especially when the pedal is used; this will enable the notes to ring out. To produce the clashing gong effects that occur in, for example, bars 9–10, the right-hand fingers can be slightly flattened, the down–up action coming mainly from the wrist. A more rounded finger-position will be needed for the low Ds in bars 52–3 (and similar places), and more of the arm weight engaged so that a deep bell-like resonance is produced, especially when the dynamic is *forte*.

There is a big dynamic range although the maximum volume marked is *forte*, so the tone when loud needs to be sufficiently moderated to allow room for the *sforzando* accents to achieve impact. In bars 19–21 and 62–4 *mezzo-forte* and *forte* should be differentiated; so it might be advisable to think of the *mezzo-forte* as closer to *mezzo-piano*. The height of the hand above the keyboard can be adjusted accordingly, thereby ensuring audible contrast. Where *pianissimo* is marked the *una corda* pedal can be engaged, as long as the tone remains focused.

Other pedalling indications have been added to the score and the footnote suggests additional use in bars 66–73 where the bars can be pedalled together in pairs according to the changing bass notes (B♭ and G). Pedal could also be added in places such as bars 46–7 to add some vibrancy to the sound. This will also aid those with smaller hands who have difficulty hanging on to the treble notes D and A, but it may be advisable to change the pedal quite rapidly to avoid an over-generous resonance.

The editorial tempo of crotchet = *c*.112 allows the music energy and momentum at a speed that is manageable for the grade. For your more extrovert students this piece provides an excellent finisher.

C:4 Valerie Capers *Mr 'Satchmo'*

This affectionate musical portrait of jazz trumpeter and singer Louis Armstrong promises to have wide appeal. Capturing the feel of this jazzy music in performance is of great importance and, as a start, the composer's request for a relaxed swing character should be heeded. An unhurried tempo can thus be adopted, perhaps in the region of crotchet = 108.

Capers helpfully instructs that the left-hand part should be played legato unless otherwise indicated, but the right-hand part seems more open to interpretation. Chordal work can be played detached, although when there are melodic fragments, as in bar 2, a more legato approach will give the upper notes an appropriate connection. A few dynamics have been written into the score but these leave scope for extra colour. For example, the last bar is marked diminuendo, but the effect can beneficially be started from around bar 35 and the 'trumpet solo' passages in bars 15–16 and 23–4 can, for a brassy effect, be played quite percussively. Both can end diminuendo so that bars 17 and 25 are played *mezzo-piano*. However, in keeping with the freer feeling of the jazz style, some nuances can be left to the performer's discretion.

Despite the potentially confusing switches between seemingly even and dotted quavers, both should be played swung so that stylistic consistency is maintained. The solo passages in bars 15–16 and 23–4 need to hold the pulse and, to this end, it may be useful to practise the triplet patterns firstly as even semiquavers. Vocalizing the swung rhythm using the scat syllables 'doo-ba-doo-ba-doo' is one way of mastering the swing feel before actually playing it. Despite the notation, the semiquavers in bar 32 may also sound better if played swung and are also more easily kept rhythmic. The silent fourth beat could trip your student up rhythmically so, as a practice measure, the tied G may be sounded (before being removed for performance).

Naturally, the best way to absorb the style is to listen to some Louis Armstrong, and his performance of *West End Blues* is a good place to start – and, in case you were wondering, Armstrong's nickname 'Satchmo' is short for 'Satchel Mouth'!

C:5 Ibert *La cage de cristal (The Crystal Cage)*

This piece is taken from a set of miniatures called 'Stories' and the title of this one suggests something finely wrought and fragile. There is much that is playfully delicate in the music but there are some richer, more songful episodes too.

Your student will need a well-defined staccato touch to play this piece effectively, especially in bars 5 and 6 (and other similar points) where fingers may be held close to the keys and pulled briskly inwards after striking to achieve an appropriate 'needlepoint' staccato. In contrast to this, the more legato passages (such as in bars 9 and 10) require a warm, deep touch with the arm weight directed towards the outer fingers of the right hand, enabling melodic projection. Conversely, in bars 21–5 arm weight will need to be focused mainly on fingers 1 and 2 if the right-hand's inner melodic part is to emerge. The dynamic levels should never be very loud and even where Ibert has marked *forte*, it would be advisable to think of this as '*f* for full' rather than '*f* for loud'. Use of the *una corda* pedal is appropriate for those passages marked *pianissimo* or quieter and will be particularly effective from bar 28 to the end.

The score indicates a number of tempo changes but it is important that a secure, basic tempo is established so that the modifications to this are telling. Crotchet = *c.*104 yields about the right speed, and one place in particular where it will be necessary to adhere strictly to the basic pulse is in bars 11 and 12. Any distortion of the timing here will weaken the gently humorous effect suggested by Ibert's use of the term *En badinant* ('in jest'). Where a ritenuto is prescribed (in bars 13 and 20) your student should ensure that the tempo modification is detectable by an examiner, perhaps exaggerating the effect as a practice measure. The final accelerando from bar 28 also needs to be carefully judged. If most of the increase in tempo is left for the penultimate bar, a premature *prestissimo* should be avoided!

This piece should suit those of your students who prefer subtlety and refinement to sound and fury.

C:6 Huw Warren *Open*

For those of your students who enjoy what Huw Warren describes as 'juicy jazzy harmonies', this piece will be an attractive option. It will also appeal to the less dextrous, because finger-work is rarely seriously challenged.

As instructed, the tempo should sound relaxed and the given metronome mark of crotchet = 112 supports this, although slightly faster or slower tempos will also work. No change to the pace is required other than where indicated in the score, and Warren warns that 'a strong sense of pulse is really essential – especially where there are no quavers.' Thus in syncopated passages such as bars 1–5 it may be beneficial to practise by tapping the beat with the foot while placing the chords in between, bodily involvement often being a helpful way of internalizing the pulse. In line with contemporary versions of R & B – one of the composer's stated influences – the quavers should not be swung.

The scored dynamics, which range from *piano* to *forte*, are precise, although this does not mean that nuances cannot be added to reflect the rise and fall of the phrases. The *forte* tone, achieved via a firm wrist and forearm, should be full but, in keeping with the relaxed style, should never sound harsh. Where *p sub* is indicated (for example in bar 17), lifting the pedal fractionally early and delaying its re-depression for a very brief moment will ensure that the dynamic drop is not obscured by sonic overhang from the previous bar. The composer has indicated where he definitely wants the pedal to be used but, in the spirit of his flexible opening suggestion, *con Ped*, there is no need to shun its use elsewhere, as long as harmonic clarity is not compromised. Articulative clarity is needed for the right-hand triplet semiquavers in bars 9, 11 and later equivalents where fingering the first two beats 2-3-2-1-3-1 might prove the strongest option.

The relative length of this piece may initially seem a little off-putting but the learning task appears less daunting when one realizes that the material of bars 7–30 is repeated, slightly reordered, in bars 31–48. In any case, the music is easily accessible and *open* to any and all!

GRADE 7

The final grades should be equally rewarding not only to the students but to the teachers and parents whose support and involvement in their development is so important. Grade 7 performances will usually sound quite accomplished at pass level, while merit and distinction categories will acknowledge musical and polished performances showing real artistic quality. The highest marks most frequently go to candidates choosing pieces within their own technical comfort zone, so that expressive details and musical communication really lift the music off the page.

A:1 C. P. E. Bach *Allegro*

This attractive final movement from one of C. P. E. Bach's early keyboard sonatas has its fair share of complexities. However, with its unexpected twists and turns, there is much to be relished by the musically inquisitive.

The pre-Classical allegro did not imply a particularly fast pace and the suggested metronome mark of crotchet = *c.*80 yields a sturdy but flowing tempo at which the faster passagework is manageable. Essentially the touch should be neat, and semiquavers can be practised in a detached manner. A more legato approach is appropriate for performance, but the sensation of the finger lifting out of the key remains important. Despite this, it is desirable to avoid a mechanical effect, and phrasing according to the contour of each passage will be musically beneficial. According to Bach's own writings, wedges and dots indicate the same staccato articulation, so there is no need for an exaggerated *staccatissimo* in bar 1 and later equivalents. Overall, the sound needs to be clean, but discreet pedalling with mainly rapid changes may aid the more legato moments, as in bar 21 and bars 44–50.

Ornaments are a significant feature of the music and the notated realizations provide valuable guidance. However, some have been adapted, and for the more adventurous, nimble-fingered student Howard Ferguson provides some useful guidance in *C. P. E. Bach Selected Keyboard Works, Book III* (ABRSM). In any case, as a practice strategy, measuring out the right-hand trill in demisemiquavers at points such as bar 12 should ensure that the left-hand semiquaver rest is not prolonged and rhythmic exactitude is preserved. In other places, trilling with fingers 4 and 2 (as in bar 68) or 3 and 1 (as in bar 31) may aid articulative clarity.

The dynamics are Bach's but it is worth remembering that *forte* on even the most powerful cembalo available to the composer would not match the level of sound possible on the modern piano, so restraint is called for. The composer largely restricts himself to *piano* and *forte* indications but other dynamic effects are implied by the music. For example, the climbing modulations in bars 13–17 and 73–7 suggest a crescendo which conveniently prepares for an echo starting on the second beat of bars 19 and 79. The rising chromatic passage in bars 53–7 similarly invites a crescendo, as does that commencing halfway through bar 24 where the marked *forte* dynamic may have to be modified.

For the theoretically minded, this piece also affords a fascinating insight into the development of sonata form.

A:2 Mozart *Allegro*

When learning Mozart's piano sonatas, it is often helpful to remember that the composer was a man of the theatre. The interpretation of this sonata-form movement might therefore benefit from imagining its contrasting musical elements as operatic characters. For example, the very opening seems polite enough but it is swiftly interrupted by a rougher voice at bar 5 which is followed by a garrulous passage from bar 11. One might imagine a daughter asking a favour from her father and receiving a gruff response, after which her mother delivers a tirade. A more yielding voice (the second subject) joins in at bar 22–3, perhaps that of a trusted family friend. The elements are then juxtaposed as if in dialogue, especially in the development section (bars 57–86) where they vie for attention. Awareness of this will help your student bring the music to life.

On a technical note, adopting a sensible tempo is one way of ensuring that finger-work remains under control and the suggested metronome mark of crotchet = *c.*108 seems judicious, although more dextrous students could raise this to *c.*116. Helpful fingerings are indicated in the score although some adaptations are possible. For example, in bar 11, to keep the hand in a single position 2-1-3-2-5-4-5-3 is viable and, for smaller hands, it may be advantageous to finger the last four right-hand semiquavers of bars 54 and 155 with 5-4-2-1, thence taking the first semiquaver of bars 55 and 156 with the left-hand thumb. Alberti-type accompaniments must be discreet and, while fingertips need to be active, they should be kept close to the keys, the wrist as still as possible.

Mozart's dynamic markings are limited to *forte*, *piano* and an occasional *pianissimo*. Naturally, the *forte* tone should never be brutal but must be strong enough to have some force especially in places such as bar 32. The *piano* of the second subject could be more delicate than the opening *piano*, the latter being more cantabile, perhaps warmed by discreet pedalling. Many of the longer runs are marked simply *forte*, but some dynamic nuances in response to the contours of the passages will guard against an unpleasantly mechanical effect. Small touches of pedal may also help to soften the edges. Mozart seems to use staccato dots and wedges interchangeably and, to reflect the humour of the music at bars 38–44 and 124–130, the grace notes are best interpreted as acciaccaturas.

Examiners will enjoy performances of this music that are seamlessly fluent (of course!), but which also realize the musical dialogues.

A:3 D. Scarlatti *Sonata in F minor*

If any composition defies the notion that minor-key music is sad, then this is it! While there is a certain urgency about the piece there is plenty of *allegrissimo* brilliance and sparkle too.

A variety of articulations will enhance the musical interest. Leaping crotchets sound convincing if executed staccato but repeated crotchets (as in bars 11–16) can be played slightly separated. The more melodic lines (as in bars 4–6) invite a legato touch while the ever-present quavers should not perhaps be played overly legato if their energy and clarity are to be preserved. The latter can be practised staccato – perhaps in the context of an F minor scale – so that the sensation of the finger always leaving the key is remembered when your student is aiming for rhythmic and articulative precision in performance.

Ornaments should ideally be delivered on the beat, using four notes and starting on the upper one. However, should this prove too problematic for your student, the style will not be compromised greatly if the ornaments are played ahead of the beat, using three notes and starting on the lower. When practising the big left-hand leaps in places such as bars 36–7, one strategy is to memorize the relevant passages, ensuring that the point at which to look back at the score is clearly identified. Another is to practise jumping the interval of an 18th in the left hand many times over while looking away from the keyboard so that gauging the distance becomes habitual.

Where dynamics are concerned this sonata offers many opportunities for echo effects but these can sometimes sound rather fussy. Another approach might be to adopt a broader view and, for example, play bars 22–34 *forte* and then bars 35–42 *piano*. After this a carefully graded crescendo will reflect the growing intensity of the passage to bar 53. A similar tactic can be used from bar 81 to the end. At the beginning *mezzo-piano* seems appropriate but a crescendo will mirror the climbing modulations of bars 11–17 after which a diminuendo will help to shape the descending scale. Generally, dynamic nuances can follow the rising and falling contours of the music.

The suggested metronome mark of dotted minim = *c.*60 yields a brisk tempo which, once underway, needs little modification. There is however scope for a minimal ritenuto in bars 52–3 and a very slightly bigger one in the closing two bars. A hair's-breadth caesura at the end of bars 21 and 80 will prepare the listener for the second subject.

A:4 Beethoven *Allegro cantabile*

Studying a composer's early work can be very illuminating, in that mature traits can sometimes be detected in embryonic form. This is certainly the case here: Beethoven's fondness for bold gestures and strong contrasts are present in this 1783 sonata movement.

However, it might be unwise to put too literal an interpretation on the dynamic markings if the music is not to sound distorted. The *piano/forte* contrasts at the opening should certainly be present but not excessively so, partly because the thin texture cannot really sustain such violence and partly because your student will need to accommodate the *fortissimo* which comes later. Even more care can be taken over the *piano/forte* in bars 11–13 and 56–8, where the *forte* need be no more than a lean on the first beat of the bar, perhaps prepared by a slight crescendo. Contrasts can be taken more at face value in bars 26–8 and 71–3. Where *fortissimo* is called for, the touch needs to be strong and decisive but, as the textures are often thin at these points, the sound can become percussive if too much force is applied.

Adopting a moderate pace allows the music overall to have space and sturdiness as required. The performance direction *Allegro cantabile* also suggests that the tempo should not be too fast – crotchet = *c.*120 seems suitable – in order that the lyrical second subject at bar 11 can sing. Careful balancing of right hand with left is required here (as elsewhere), allowing adequate depth to the touch in the right hand while keeping the left-hand fingers as close to the keys as possible, engaging only minimal movement.

The trickiest fingering occurs in bars 23–4, where an awkward right-hand manoeuvre can be eased by taking the F at the beginning of bar 24 with the thumb of the left hand – and similarly the B♭ in bar 69.

Continuous pedalling is not necessary but discreet use of the sustaining pedal may be beneficial. For example, its use can add lustre to the *forte* chords in bars 1–3 and 31–3, and can aid connectivity in the *piano* phrases during bars 26–30 and 71–5. Its engagement may also add resonance to the arpeggio passages in bars 48–52, although it might be advisable to change with each beat, or at least every two beats, to ensure clarity.

For those who relish drama and who shy away from continuous runs, this is a welcome syllabus inclusion which can provide a positive start to an exam recital programme.

A:5 Handel *Allemande*

Though perhaps undeservedly neglected, the keyboard suites by Handel contain some real charmers such as this allemande from his Suite in D minor, HWV 449. No huge demands on keyboard agility are made but the music calls for subtlety of articulation and tone control.

Writing in 1739, Johann Mattheson described the allemande as 'serious ... and delighting in order and calm'. Thus a tempo can be adopted which allows an elegant but unhurried flow, and crotchet = *c.*72 would work well. Engaging a firm but pliant touch, the upper melodic parts can move in a generally legato manner although leaping left-hand quavers (as in bars 5 and 9) may be lightly detached, as may accompanying quavers that fall between the beats (as in bars 1 and 3). Where left-hand quavers have a melodic role to play (as in bar 3), then legato playing seems more appropriate.

Small hands will struggle to keep the legato connections at points such as beats 3–4 of bars 4 and 7 in the upper parts. In these instances it may be necessary to use the thumb or another finger on two consecutive notes and to rely on deft pedalling to cover the break, as long as there is no resultant blurring. Shorter trills can include up to six notes. For example, on the first beat of bar 20 a suitable pattern is G-F-G-F-E-F, leading on to the G of beat 2. Where the lowest note of the trill is a black note (as in bar 17, end of beat 3), fingering 3-1-3-1-2-3 with the fifth finger on the first E of beat 4 may provide a suitably positive articulation.

Dynamically, you might consider opening the music *mezzo-piano* and applying a crescendo in bars 8 and 9, reaching *forte* in bar 10. The second half presents more opportunities for rise and fall which can be effectively realized in several ways. For example, starting *piano* in bar 18, there might then be a crescendo to bar 20, a diminuendo in bar 22 and a final crescendo in the second half of bar 23, concluding the piece at a healthy *forte*. It should however be remembered that all the right-hand passagework needs a sense of contour through tonal nuance and to this end a semiquaver subsequent to a tie (as in bar 2, beats 2 and 4) needs to ease in the ensuing phrase and should never be unduly emphasized. Rubato may also be discreetly applied to reflect cadence points in bars 7–8 and 14 as well as, more obviously, just before the double bar-line and at the end.

A:6 Paradies *Presto*

The Italian composer Paradies is mainly known for his Toccata in A, a movement from one of his sonatas, but this Presto (from another sonata) shows that the Toccata is not the only attractive keyboard music written by this little-known composer.

It is worth remembering that in the eighteenth century 'presto' did not carry the implications of extreme velocity that it subsequently acquired, so while the music must certainly move it need not rush. A metronome mark in the region of crotchet = 88–100 should yield an appropriate momentum. It may also be noted that the last semiquaver in bar 22 should almost certainly be a G♮.

As with all 'moto perpetuo'-type music, a good fingering is of paramount importance, especially as ornaments have to be integrated. The trills may justifiably be executed as mordents and it would be wise to arrange the fingering so that stronger fingers are engaged. For example, in bar 1 and later equivalents the following will work: 2-1-3-2-5-3-232-1, and in bar 3 and later equivalents the following may be helpful: 3-5-1-4-3-2-121-2. It is also worth trying 535 for the inverted mordents (rather than 545) because stronger fingers promote clearer articulation.

Generally the touch needs to sparkle, with the left-hand quavers played either lightly detached or possibly with the first quaver of the bar slurred on to the second. When practising the right-hand semiquavers, the sensation of lifting the fingers upwards is at least as important as that of going down into the key. Slow, staccato practice can be used to develop the necessary sense of lift, and, while playing the right-hand passagework staccato at a fast speed would be inappropriate (not to mention impossible!), the muscular memory of active fingers bred by staccato practice will be beneficial.

Played on the piano, the inclusion of dynamics will aid the musical effect and guard against tonal monotony. For example, from a general *piano/mezzo-piano* level, crescendos may be applied in bars 6–10 and 24–31, and these may be followed by an easing off during bars 12–20 and 45–55. As with all quite lengthy crescendos, careful grading is required to ensure that the summit is not reached too soon, leaving an ugly forcing of the tone as the only option for producing further volume. Most of the crescendo can be left until the last bar or two. (Similar thinking in reverse will apply to lengthy diminuendos.)

This music certainly needs dextrous fingers and rhythmic stability but, once these essentials are mastered, the piece is a delight to play and to listen to.

B:1 Bridge *Berceuse*

The simplicity and charm of this lullaby will make it a popular choice. A lovely singing tone, reliable pedalling and confidence in handling two against three are the main requirements.

This piece was originally written for the violin, so it would be helpful to imagine a violin sound while playing the melody. The dynamics should be built in from the start – they follow the shape of the phrasing and give it expression. The left hand has most of the accompaniment, and for the first 12 bars the hand pivots on F. It is possible to use third finger on this note throughout these bars, or to use second for the first four bars and third for the next eight. This will give the hand a sense of anchorage as it swings gently from side to side.

Much of the first section is underpinned by a tonic pedal note, and, except for a handful of bars, the pedal only needs to be changed on first beats. Where there are widely spread chords (as in bars 17 and 35) care should be taken that the bass note is caught by the pedal – this means making the change slightly earlier than usual. The stretch in bar 76 will be beyond most hands, so the bass note should be treated as though it is an acciaccatura and the A and E♭ above taken with the left hand (second finger and thumb). This leaves the right hand with only the interval of a 7th. In the previous bar the pedal can be released after the first beat, allowing the melody G♭ to sing alone; then there will be no difficulty in catching the bass note of the next bar.

Like so many lullabies, the middle section becomes disturbed – baby is restless. The tempo moves a little quicker (*Poco più mosso*), but as the accompaniment changes to triplets only a slight increase in speed will be needed. Now the pedal changes with every beat until arriving at *molto ritard*. There should be no hint of jerkiness as the melody flows over the triplets, so if the technique of two against three is new to your student it is worthwhile devising some preliminary exercises before proceeding. The passage from bar 45 to bar 52 is further complicated by spread chords, so it might help to practise them without spreading until the rhythm feels secure. This may result in temporarily omitting the lowest note of the widest chords (bars 47 and 50).

Fragments of the melody are given to the left hand towards the end (bars 77–82), and the *una corda* pedal from bar 89 will help the music to fade as the baby sleeps at last.

B:2 Liszt *Piano Piece in F sharp*

One look at the key signature may be enough to deter some, and a second glance at all the accidentals will probably only strengthen their resolve to try something else! This beautiful piece is certainly not for the faint-hearted, but for those that tackle it there are rich rewards to be reaped.

The left hand sets the scene with an undulating pattern which is repeated with only a few alterations. If preferred, fingers 5-2-1-3-1-2-1-3-2 can be used for this figure. The third finger acts as a pivot and this sequence will work for most of the first 13 bars. In bars 4 and 10 the fourth finger should be used as the pivot. The right-hand part of the first page is relatively straightforward until it comes to fitting it with the accompaniment. Then a secure grasp of two against three will be essential.

Look before you play is the best advice for the middle section. The plethora of accidentals on the second page is really not as frightening as it seems. The chromatic figures in bars 15 and 17 are all major 3rds, and, while Liszt's fingerings indicate the detached manner in which to play them, a more modern fingering will help to locate the notes more safely. After the held G major chord in bar 15, fingers 3/2, 4/1, 3/1, 4/2, 3/1, arriving with 4/2 on the first beat of bar 16, can be used – in bar 17 similarly, but with an extra 3/2 and 4/1 at the beginning of the group. For the right hand of bar 22 Liszt's own fingering is the only one that works, and a good fingering is provided for the left hand.

The final section is back in the calm waters of the home key. After the excitement of the chromaticism in the middle section, the mood becomes dreamy. However, while the left hand has much less to do, the right is now more elaborately decorated, and here a word of caution should be given. The player with smaller hands may find some of the stretches and the continual movement of the extended hand a strain. The hand should be kept as loose as possible assisted by a little forearm rotation.

Rubato is essential to shape the phrasing and point out special moments in the harmony, like the sudden appearances of the G major chord in bars 15 and 17. There are also other indications for tempo change that add to the ebb and flow of this Romantic music.

B:3 Schubert *Scherzo and Trio*

There is plenty of action in this exciting, but sometimes whimsical, movement. Schubert's unexpected harmonies and modulations never fail to surprise and delight.

It could be practised slowly hands together right from the beginning. Just a few passages (e.g. bars 25–8; 65–9) would benefit from some separate-hands study. However, it will eventually need a quick tempo, and it is important that the techniques employed can be speeded up without strain. Practising a 'slowed-down fast version' is the key to success. It should be borne in mind that the editor's metronome speed (dotted minim = *c*.72) is an approximate guide; it will still sound effective several notches lower.

Articulation is all-important. The three-note motto – two quavers and minim – pervades and drives the Scherzo. The quavers need precision and clarity with the second one slurred as marked, and the minim held for its full two beats. Very little pedal is required in the Scherzo, but it will be useful for joining some chords and reinforcing the tone in places: the minim in bar 4; from the third beat of bar 8 to the second in bar 9 (changing on the first beat); from the second beat of bar 10 to the first of bar 11, and so on. The descending crotchet octaves in bar 11 and many of the crotchet chords will be detached. However others, like those in bars 40–41, would benefit from brief touches of pedal to add force while still allowing them to sound detached.

The graceful Trio makes a striking contrast. A little slower and almost always quiet, it is as though heard from a distance or as a memory. The *una corda* pedal instruction applies to the whole section including the *mezzo-forte* passage, and legato pedalling is essential. Some of the left-hand chords may appear tricky (bars 142–5 and similar), but, using the second finger on C as an anchor, these can be spread lightly. It would be a good idea to memorize the last eight bars so that the hand-crossing can be watched.

Once the movement is technically secure and the tempo beginning to move, the quirky effect of the held chords (e.g. bars 13–14 and 17–18) followed by sudden bursts of speed can be enjoyed. Full value should always be given to tied notes and rests, especially in bars 54–7. In bars 40–41 there could be a very slight pulling-up on those big chords. Conversely, the puckish character of this Scherzo suggests that the closing bars (from bar 120) should hurtle forwards to the final bars.

B:4 Elgar *Andantino*

The dream children of this wistful piece are a figment of the writer Charles Lamb's imagination – the children he never had. There are two versions, one for solo piano and the other for orchestra, and Elgar placed a quotation from Lamb's essay at the top of his score: '...We are nothing; less than nothing, and dreams. *We are only what might have been...*'

This is a piece for the pianist with imagination, a sure sense of rubato and reliable pedal technique. Listening to the orchestral version could provide your student with ideas for sonority and colour, but the orchestral version might be played slower than is advisable for the piano. The opening bar can be used to set the tempo if the performer mentally sings the first bar of the melody as the octave is held. The given metronome mark may feel slightly fast for managing the chords, but it should not be much slower than around dotted crotchet = 44.

A quite lavish use of legato pedalling will be required, and the markings provided in the first few bars give a clue as to how to proceed elsewhere. However, after the pause in bars 6 and 21 the slurred groups of three quavers need tiny breaks between them, so direct pedalling will be needed there. Where the composer asks for *ppp* it would be sensible to employ the *una corda* pedal, too.

Although the pedalling marked for bars 13 and 14 may suggest that the silent replacing of thumb with fifth finger on the left hand's tied notes is unnecessary, this technique will encourage a smooth movement and note-security for the next chord. However, unless the hand-stretch is large, bar 16 will need some skilful co-ordination of left hand and pedal. The first low E♭ may be played as an acciacciatura before the other two notes. The pedal will have to be changed halfway through the bar, but not until the fifth finger has silently retaken the bass note again, so good use of the *rit.* should be made here.

Rubato must not be allowed to distort the phrasing, but the composer has indicated how flexible the tempo should be, by scattering through the score such directions as *ten.*, *molto lento*, *rit.* and *a tempo*. These should all be meticulously observed. Plenty of time should be taken in bar 8 with the *molto lento* and pause; the crescendo from *pianissimo* to *forte* and back again needs space. Similarly, the performer should take time at the end, as the music dissolves onto a major chord and the image of the children fades away.

B:5 Grovlez *Berceuse de la poupée (Lullaby of the Doll)*

Here is an opportunity to dip into Grovlez's wonderfully descriptive world of childhood. In the poem by Tristan Klingsor that inspired this lullaby, the child tells bedtime stories as she sings her doll to sleep.

Grovlez, like Debussy before him, uses the popular French lullaby, '*Do, do, l'enfant do,*' and the rhythmic pattern of two crotchets, two quavers and crotchet can be heard in more than a third of the piece – sometimes with altered intervals and in bars 20–21 in inversion. A good exercise would be to ask your student to search for them and mark them in the score.

Pedals play an important part in helping to contrast the simplicity of the opening theme with the magical, sometimes eerie passages or 'stories' that disturb the calm of the lullaby. At first normal legato pedalling, changing every beat, will keep the texture transparent, but at bar 11 (also bars 16 and 67) the pedal must be held for three bars, allowing the pedal note E♭ to resonate under the mysterious harmony and fleeting figures above – the shadowy cats on the roof that are alluded to in the poem, perhaps? The *una corda* pedal is used in many of these capricious phrases, adding further contrast to the more reassuring rocking figures.

At bar 30 a clock begins to strike (left-hand minims), and the excitement rises. This passage should begin very quietly and make a steady crescendo so that the long pedal effects remain viable. The pace of pedal changes will increase as the harmony becomes more chromatic, and care should be taken over accuracy of notes. The right hand has a mix of major and minor 3rds under the melody in bars 34–7, but changes to chromatically moving minor 3rds until fading into the calmness of the rocking motif again at bar 44.

Fingering is not a problem, but where the hands cross in bars 5–8 the left should be kept above the right. In bars 20 and 21 it would be helpful to use fingers 3/2 for the right-hand pair of notes (D/C); they will then act as a pivot between the revolving A♭ octaves. A musical performance will demonstrate the ability to etch out melody notes from the chords: for instance, the inner notes of the first two bars and upper ones in the next. A fine control of dynamics will also be essential. Apart from the climax in the middle section and a brief *mezzo-forte* in bar 46, subtle shades of quiet playing between *p* and *pppp* must be found – not easy when playing an unfamiliar piano.

B:6 Tchaikovsky *März (March)*

March would still be a cold month in Russia, so the skylark of the subtitle (Song of the Lark) would be a most welcome harbinger of the longed-for spring. Nevertheless, since an air of melancholy pervades this beautiful piece, it may be more a case of wishful thinking.

It is often difficult to decide just how much pedal to use in passages where one hand has staccato or rests, while the other clearly needs to be sustained and enriched. In Romantic music compromises often have to be made, and this piece is a case in point. Taking the view that legato pedalling is the norm, it would be wise to take note of passages that require staccato, or 'breaths' at phrase-endings. For instance, bars 5–6 might be better without pedal, firstly to allow a breath after the first quaver and secondly so that the melody, now in the bass, is not blurred. It is also worth noting that in some editions the right-hand chords of these bars are marked with staccato dots.

The slurred staccato in bar 10 could be treated either with or without pedal according to taste. However, the middle section is marked *un pochettino più mosso*, indicating a change of mood. The skylark's song rises with the staccato semiquavers, and bars 11–12 should ideally be without pedal. Fortunately the accompaniment here can be easily sustained with the fingers, but from the second half of bar 17 into bar 19 pedal may well be needed to join the wider spacing of the chords and B♭pedal notes. The warbling figures with their chirruping acciaccaturas should still be played with a staccato touch, though.

A metronome mark of crotchet = *c*.52 will allow the *Andantino espressivo* to unfold persuasively – the Russian mood of nostalgia should be very much in evidence – and the quaintly expressed *pochettino* ('very little') increase in speed should be kept in proportion. Decorative figures and ornamentation that represent the lark's song should always be rhythmic, but rubato will be needed to shape the phrases and give expression. There can be a little lingering on appoggiaturas (second beats of bars 4 and 10, for instance). Encourage your student to feel the ebb and flow of the music, but without exaggeration, of course.

At bar 31 the first theme returns exactly as before, but even more forlorn after the birdsong has faded. The coda begins at bar 39 and *una corda* pedal will help the effect of dying away as the melody gradually fragments into silence.

C:1 Ginastera *Danza de la moza donosa (Dance of the Graceful Young Girl)*

There surely exists no more beautiful piece than this dance with its wonderful range of melancholic and passionate emotions. The intense ardour of the middle section, complemented by a beginning and ending of utter simplicity and plaintiveness, creates a perfect arch-like shape.

The two-in-a-bar lilting rhythmic figure stated in the first bar continues almost unaltered throughout the piece. While lifting the pedal only once per bar ensures that the harmonies are sustained, the ear will judge when the harmonic complexity requires an additional half-pedal change midway through the bar. A velvet smooth left-hand texture at the start, with fingers close to the keys and slightly highlighted thumb notes, will immediately set the scene for the right-hand *cantando* love-song. This expressive guitar-like melody suggests its own gentle shape, which can be enhanced by equally subtle rhythmic ebb and flow. The addition of a second right-hand 'voice' at bar 12 adds an eight-bar glimpse of the intensity which is to follow. The tone becomes warmer here and both lines have an importance to be savoured as they interweave chromatically.

The composer's carefully considered dynamic markings provide the clue to managing the long crescendo towards the climax at bar 49. Starting this middle section as quietly as possible and not becoming over-loud too soon are the keys to success here. Quavers should be joined with the fingers wherever possible, in addition to using the pedal, to ensure a smooth left-hand harmonic 'cushion' over which the right hand sings its increasingly ardent song. The unusual mixture of sonorities created by the right-hand 4ths and 5ths from bar 24 is further enriched by the introduction of four-note chords later on. The left hand needs confidence at this point as it strides over the keyboard, and a keen eye will ensure correct right-hand accidentals.

Initially the overall shape of the right hand from bar 40 can be established by practising the octaves without the inner notes, after which spreading the four-note chords upwards will help the ear to register the chromatic clusters. Arm weight supported by a supple wrist will achieve full richness and tonal warmth at the loudest levels and the impetuous, yet emphatic mood can be enhanced by pushing the quavers forward towards the climax.

A steeply graded diminuendo leads back to the mood of the opening. Using the *una corda* pedal from bar 59 onwards will enhance the sense of poignancy as the right hand, this time in 3rds, sings its distant song. The alto dotted minims further intensify the atmosphere and the quasi-improvised guitar arpeggio provides a dreamlike stillness to the ending.

C:2 Schoenberg *Leicht, zart (Lightly, delicately)*

Although this piece may appear an unappealing choice at first sight, it is worth considering for an intelligent, enterprising student with a keen eye for accidentals and an ability to cope with complex rhythms. The atonal style may seem strange and unfamiliar to begin with, but after the ear has become attuned to the lack of a key centre, the rich melodic beauty and wealth of original ideas start to emerge.

Initially subdividing the main beats into quaver units, perhaps marking their exact position on the score, is a valuable starting-point for understanding the rhythmic structure. Faster notes, rests and syncopations need particular care. However, once this groundwork has been achieved, the mathematics must give way to thinking in larger units in order to allow the phrases to flow naturally. Notice also the composer's meticulous tempo instructions which should be absorbed into the overall structure, with care always being taken to return to the original pace after any diversion.

The frequent changes of clef need close scrutiny, and careful listening will help your student to appreciate the musical effect of the many accidentals. Naturals often act simply as reminders of cancelled flats or sharps, and ties across enharmonically altered notes in bars 3 and 14 should not be missed.

Although there is a fragmentary, almost cinematic quality to many of the ideas, the harmonic and melodic style is essentially rooted in post-

Wagnerian Romanticism. Phrases may seem short and somewhat insubstantial, yet warmth and affection are needed to project the melodic strands as they shift between registers. The linear texture may be best understood by thinking in orchestral terms – for instance, a flute might play the wispy figure in bar 8 and the mellow sonority of the *espressivo* tenor line in bars 4–5 may be assigned to the French horn.

Schoenberg's detailed dynamics and hairpins leave us in no doubt regarding phrase inflection. Good key control is needed to explore different levels of quiet tone, especially when on occasion the hands are given opposing instructions. The *fpp* outburst appears as something of a surprise in bar 8 after which the tremolo, which should be in measured demisemiquavers finishing at the middle of bar 10, acts as a musical reverberation. Other notable musical 'effects' include the dotted left-hand figures punctuated by short chords in bar 7 and the striking shift of register at bar 15.

Selective use of the pedal will add warmth to the sustained phrases. However, frequent changes are essential for melodic clarity and pedal must not obscure the rests. The addition of the *una corda* pedal will add further colour to the ending.

C:3 Shostakovich *Allegretto*

Here one senses the young Shostakovich establishing himself as the writer of light-hearted, witty music. The elusive, fleeting ideas and almost balletic rhythms give the piece a charm and nonchalance and, although we are given glimpses of C major at certain points, the ambiguous harmonies prevent full assertion of the tonality until the final bars.

The two main thematic ideas which recur in various guises throughout the piece are introduced in the first four bars. Sustaining the harmonies with the fingers in bars 1–2 allows clarity to the gentle right-hand slurs, which need incisive rhythm. Use of the pedal in the two bars that follow creates a richer harmonic texture as the right-hand figures sweep arch-like over the keyboard. Fluent ease of movement is reliant on a light arm and the hand-positions can be established by practising in 'block' shapes. After the perfect cadence, albeit a slightly quirky one, in bar 8, the sustained chords of the following bar suggest a more pensive mood. However, the skittish descending figures soon shatter any seriousness. Rhythm needs care here, with the rests clearly shown, and observance of the meticulously graded dynamics will effect a steep diminuendo.

Bar 13 sees the start of a six-bar build-up towards the climax of the piece. Again, the light-hearted rising figures ensure that the mood does not remain serious for long. The descending chromatic melodic lines need prominence and clean pedalling, and confident sideways movement of the arms and upper body will ensure that the triplets flow with ease. Your student should check the A♮ (not A♭) which forms an augmented chord in bar 14. A sense of urgency is created by the harmonic shifts twice per bar from bar 17. Memorizing this section allows the attention to be focused fully on the keyboard as the hands spring off the first- and third-beat chords in order to move to the next position. Good articulation will give full impact to the short crescendos, and the octaves in bar 19 need a steely brilliance provided by firm fingers and supportive arm weight. The feeling of suspense and theatrical gesture can be enjoyed by giving full value to the rests which follow.

The C major tonality becomes more firmly established from bar 25 onwards. Slightly emphasizing the semitone shifts in the bass line adds colour to the harmonies. The change of figuration midway through bar 27 needs care, and all notes must sound in the pizzicato-like chords (bars 29–30). Carefully paced rests in the penultimate bar and the quietest tone will allow the piece to creep stealthily away.

C:4 Gershwin *Do It Again*

This delicious transcription with its scrumptious harmonies and subtle pianistic voicing seems to transport us from the exam room to the cocktail bar. Gershwin's ability to convey the spirit of song within a convincing piano idiom is masterly here. Dynamics meticulously document any subtleties of voicing, and musical interest is provided by imaginative use of keyboard registers.

A good performance should contain all the beauty of the finest Romantic playing yet evoke the sophisticated charm and nonchalance of the inter-war years. This suave, polished cocktail style relies on subtle ebb and flow to the rhythm in order to preserve its musical flow, and thinking in minim rather than crotchet beats will help create that all-important laid-back expansiveness to the phrasing. Careful listening will guide pedalling choices; changing only twice per bar works well in many places, although quicker harmonic shifts will require more frequent releasing of the pedal. A similarly keen eye will ensure that the large number of accidentals is correct, and a comfortable octave span is advantageous when negotiating the chord-patterns.

The main vocal line, which begins at the first chord, can be traced throughout the piece. Singing this line at a convenient pitch is the best way to discover its natural shape and inflection. Firm tone from the little finger will allow the right-hand A to sustain while the tenor 'voice' weaves the first of its beguiling countermelodies. The delicious G♯/G♮ clash in bar 2 provides the first glimpse of the wonderful chromaticisms to which we are treated throughout. At bars 5–6 the triplets, which can be quite flexible in rhythm, seem to pull against the straight crotchets. Your student must make sure that all melodic notes project clearly here. The register-change as the melody moves up the octave creates a new, more elated mood as the crescendo reaches upwards to the first climax of the piece. The chromatic tenor line, if subtly accented, contributes to the enjoyment here and the opportunity to linger on arrival at bar 11 should not be missed. The allargando in bar 16 allows space for the left-hand figures (which need judicious fingering) to be negotiated comfortably. In addition, careful pedalling will enable the grace notes to be sustained.

Many of the ideas presented up to this point reappear in the second half, this time yet more inventively textured. Further development of voicing takes place – the quaver inner line at the approach to the piece's second climax at bar 27 is particularly lovely – and subtle control of tone will ensure that the main musical lines remain clearly projected above and within the rich chords.

C:5 Christopher Norton *Sturdy Build*

'Sternly' is not a word usually applied to music, yet it seems to sum up perfectly the persistent, feisty character of this piece. Its flamboyance and constant rhythmic drive make it best suited to a confident student who has flair and a largish hand to manage the stretchy chords and octave passages.

A firm sense of pulse, equal to that of the best 'jazzer', is essential for managing the piece's numerous rhythmic challenges. Identifying exactly where the four main beats occur is a good starting-point for understanding the syncopations. Simultaneously tapping the right-hand printed rhythm with one hand while maintaining the pulse with the other may be a valuable additional exercise. Thereafter, as always in this style, the rhythm must be 'felt' in order to flow convincingly, as if improvised. The octaves and wide leaps on the final page are the clue to the best choice of tempo, which must be sustainable through to the last bar.

Clearly defined right-hand slurs, firm and well accented, will immediately set the mood in the opening. The lower register and quieter dynamic of the next bar create a musical subtext, a pattern which is repeated at each statement of this idea. A smooth line can be conveyed by joining the top notes of the right-hand chords at bar 9, using a combination of fourth and fifth fingers, to contrast with the more spiky left-hand phrasing.

Arm weight, keeping the wrist supple, will produce sonorous tone in the *fortissimo* chords at bar 17. Ideally these bars should be memorized in order to allow concentration on managing the leaps accurately and with 'spot-on' rhythmic precision. Additional sonority is created by the pedal, but care is needed to clear it fully at the change of harmony.

The 7/8 bar creates an interesting rhythmic irregularity, which can be further highlighted by punchy accents in the following bars. Your student shouldn't miss the opportunity to emphasize the bass octaves at bar 25.

Bar 29 sees the start of a reprise of the opening music, this time filled out with octaves and large chords. Really punchy left-hand accents and sharply delineated phrasing will underline the rock style here. The repeated octaves beginning in bar 37 can be facilitated by using a wrist action, and thumb notes of the four-note right-hand chords may be omitted if the stretch is unmanageable. Confidence over the keyboard is needed to keep bars 43–7 moving rhythmically. The length of tied notes should be checked here and the music kept driving forward until the final *sec.* octave.

C:6 Prokofiev *Con vivacità*

One can sense the young Prokofiev setting out to shock his audience with this quirky music, with its outer sections full of short jagged phrases and unexpected accents and, sandwiched in between, eight bars of music which seem to inhabit a completely different world.

The metronomically regular left-hand staccato crotchets and accents on less important beats create a balletic feel to the start – albeit a somewhat lopsided one. Holding the dotted quavers for their full value, with the demisemiquavers cleanly articulated, will establish the rhythmic structure. It should be noticed that the whole section is predominantly quiet, with only a couple of *forte* outbursts. While the accents serve to highlight the deliberately ambiguous rhythmic patterns, they should be tempered according to the *piano* dynamic. Tapering the ends of the short phrases will add further character to the phrasing. Although the left hand plays a largely accompanimental role here, firm fingers are needed to ensure that all chord notes sound. Attention can be focused on the keyboard if the more awkward leaps are memorized, and some chord accidentals may need special care, especially the B♯ in bar 9.

The final two bars of the section are likely to prove the most challenging in the piece. Here confident, fluent movement is needed, with the thumbs accurately placed, as the hands travel in opposite directions across the keyboard. Practising the figuration in block chords may help to secure the patterns. Light, airy tone, without any hint of a crescendo, will give maximum contrast to the sudden accent, and a little pedal might enhance the slur; elsewhere in the section, however, a drier texture seems to be called for.

The change of key heralds a calmer, if somewhat mysterious, mood. The melody in octaves creates a hauntingly eerie effect as this folksong weaves gently around, its *espressivo* character highlighted by a more flexible rhythmic approach than elsewhere. The contours of each of its two four-bar phrases suggest their own tonal rise and fall, which must be sufficiently subtle to maintain the calm atmosphere within a *pianissimo* context. Its quartet-like texture with smooth, bowed first violin and viola lines contrasting with yet quieter pizzicato second violin and cello interjections can be conveyed here by careful fingering and good control of tone.

The smallest hint of a broadening of tempo allows the mood to slip back to that of the opening, this time still quieter and more delicate. Keeping close to the keys will allow good control of the detail at a whispered dynamic, thus heightening the effect of the bold closing gesture.